LAPTOPS
Simplified®

Visual

by Kate Shoup

WILEY

Wiley Publishing, Inc.

LAPTOPS SIMPLIFIED®

Published by
Wiley Publishing, Inc.
10475 Crosspoint Boulevard
Indianapolis, IN 46256

www.wiley.com

Published simultaneously in Canada

Library of Congress Control Number is available from the Publisher upon request.

ISBN: 978-0-470-76902-7

Manufactured in the United States of America

10 9 8 7 6 5 4 3 2 1

Trademark Acknowledgments

Contact Us

For general information on our other products and services please contact our Customer Care Department within the U.S. at 877-762-2974, outside the U.S. at 317-572-3993 or fax 317-572-4002.

For technical support please visit www.wiley.com/techsupport.

Permissions

Mike Agassi and Dominic Cobello from *"The Agassi Story"*
Kate Bova
Jennie DeVoe
David Huss
Barbara Shoup

Wiley Publishing, Inc.

Sales

Contact Wiley at (877) 762-2974 or fax (317) 572-4002.

Credits

Acquisitions Editor
Aaron Black

Project Editor
Jade L. Williams

Technical Editor
Vince Averello

Copy Editor
Scott Tullis

Editorial Director
Robyn Siesky

Editorial Manager
Rosemarie Graham

Business Manager
Amy Knies

Senior Marketing Manager
Sandy Smith

**Vice President and
Executive Group Publisher**
Richard Swadley

**Vice President and
Executive Publisher**
Barry Pruett

Project Coordinator
Patrick Redmond

**Graphics and Production
Specialists**
Joyce Haughey
Andrea Hornberger
Jennifer Mayberry

Proofreading
Henry Lazarek

Indexing
Potomac Indexing, LLC

Screen Artists
Ana Carrillo
Jill A. Proll
Ronald Terry

About the Author

Kate Shoup has authored more than 20 books and edited scores more. Recent titles include *Office 2010 Simplified*, *Teach Yourself Visually Office 2010*, *Windows 7 Digital Classroom*, *Teach Yourself Visually Outlook 2007*, *Office 2007: Top 100 Simplified Tips & Tricks*, and *Internet Visual Quick Tips*. She has also co-written a feature-length screenplay (and starred in the ensuing film) and worked as the Sports Editor for *NUVO Newsweekly*. When not working, Kate loves to ski (she was once nationally ranked), read, ride her motorcycle, and follow the IndyCar circuit — and she plays a mean game of 9-ball. Kate lives in Indianapolis with her daughter, her SO, and their dog.

Author's Acknowledgments

Thanks go out to publisher Barry Pruett and to acquisitions editor Aaron Black for giving me the opportunity to tackle this exciting project. Even more thanks go to project editor Jade Williams for her dedication and patience in guiding this project from start to finish. Thanks to copy editor Scott Tullis, who ensured that all the i's were dotted and t's were crossed, and to technical editor Vince Averello, who skillfully checked each step and offered valuable input along the way. Thanks to the production team at Wiley for their able efforts in creating such a visual masterpiece. Many thanks and much love to my beautiful and brilliant daughter, Heidi Welsh; to my incredible parents, Barb and Steve Shoup; to my wonderful sister, Jenny Shoup; to my brother-in-law, Jim Plant; to my nephew, Jake Plant; and to *mon ti lapin*, Francois Dubois.

How to Use This Book

Who This Book Is For

This book is for the reader who has never used this particular technology or software application. It is also for readers who want to expand their knowledge.

The Conventions in This Book

1 Steps

This book uses a step-by-step format to guide you easily through each task. Numbered steps are actions you must do; bulleted steps clarify a point, step, or optional feature; and indented steps give you the result.

2 Notes

Notes give additional information — special conditions that may occur during an operation, a situation that you want to avoid, or a cross reference to a related area of the book.

3 Icons and Buttons

Icons and buttons show you exactly what you need to click to perform a step.

4 Simplify It

Simplify It sections offer additional information, including warnings and shortcuts.

5 Bold

Bold type shows command names, options, and text or numbers you must type.

6 Italics

Italic type introduces and defines a new term.

Table of Contents

1

Choosing Your Laptop PC

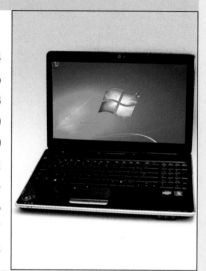

2

Setting Up Your Laptop PC

3

Using Software Programs on Your Laptop PC

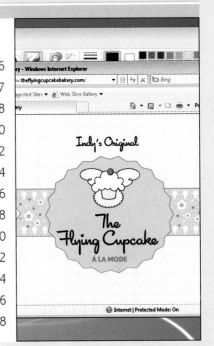

4

Navigating Files and Folders in Windows 7

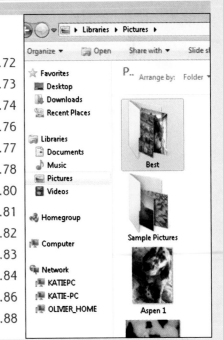

Table of Contents

5

Working with Images on Your Laptop PC

6

Enjoying Audio and Video on Your Laptop

7

Word Processing in Windows 7

8

Exploring the Internet and the World Wide Web with Your Laptop

Table of Contents

9

Getting Organized with Your Laptop

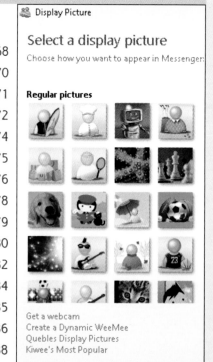

10

Staying in Touch

Networking Your Laptop PC

Maintaining Your Laptop PC

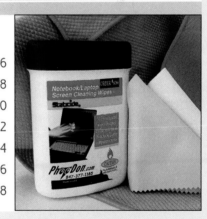

Securing Your Laptop PC

Chapter 1

Choosing Your Laptop PC

Portable computers, generally referred to as *laptops* or *notebooks*, began as a great tool for people who traveled and wanted to bring their computer along. Today, laptops with high-end displays and huge processing power are taking over the desktop, as well.

Although laptop models vary by weight, size, keyboard configuration, and more, they share some common traits. For example, on a laptop, the keyboard, pointing device, and monitor are built-in.

Like their desktop counterparts, laptop computers run an operating system (OS). The most commonly used OS is Windows. Computers that run Windows are generally referred to as *PCs*, which stands for *personal computers*.

Explore a Laptop

Laptop computers are very similar to their desktop counterparts. Both contain a hard drive and other hardware. Both use an operating system, run software, and save files. And both can be connected to peripheral devices such as printers.

Key differences exist, however. For example, laptops, which are designed for portability, are much more compact. In addition, whereas desktops require an external keyboard and mouse, these features along with a monitor are built into laptops (although you can plug in a standard keyboard or mouse if desired). Finally, laptops can run on a battery, whereas desktops require an electrical outlet.

Monitor
The monitor on a laptop is typically made of a soft-to-the-touch, and somewhat fragile, liquid crystal display.

Keyboard
Keyboard configurations vary based on the size of the laptop, with larger laptops having a separate number pad and smaller ones embedding number-pad functionality within the regular keys.

Touchpad Pointing Device
Laptops feature a built-in pointing device — usually a touchpad, as shown here. You move your finger over the pad to move the mouse pointer on your screen.

Function Keys
Most laptops have preassigned functions for these aptly named function keys. Typical uses are for muting the speakers or accessing the Internet.

DVD Drive

Most laptops include a DVD drive, although some still feature a CD drive. The location of these drives varies by model.

Battery

A battery usually slots into the bottom of a laptop. This battery needs to be recharged on a regular basis.

Power-Cord Connector

To recharge your battery, you plug in your laptop using a power-cord connector.

Explore Slots and Ports

You can use the various slots and ports built into your laptop to connect peripheral devices to it, such as a printer, a mouse, a keyboard, an extra monitor, headphones, a microphone, a digital camera, and more. Most of these slots and ports are located on the sides or back of the laptop.

Note that in addition to using the slots and ports built into your laptop to connect peripheral devices, you can also connect these devices to ports and slots in a docking station. You can then plug your laptop into the docking station to access the peripheral devices.

USB Port

You can use a universal serial bus (USB) port to connect a wide variety of devices, from a flash drive for data storage to a printer or digital camera. Devices that can be connected via USB are generally plug-and-play — that is, you need not restart your computer to use them after connecting them via a USB cable. And Windows can automatically install many USB devices when you connect them, requiring no additional input from you.

Memory Card Reader

A memory card is a small, removable digital storage device used in many electronic gadgets such as digital cameras, MP3 players, and so on. Many laptops feature memory card readers — small slots into which you can insert a memory card. You can then view the contents of the memory card, and even use the memory card as an external storage device to save data on your laptop.

Monitor Port

Some laptop computers include a monitor port. If you want to connect an external monitor to your laptop — for example, to show a presentation on a larger screen or if you use a dual-monitor system in your workflow — you can connect a standard monitor cable into the laptop's monitor port.

Ethernet Jack

You use an Ethernet jack to connect your computer to a router that controls your local area network (LAN) through a coaxial or fiber-optic cable. You can also use an Ethernet jack to establish a high-speed connection to the Internet. You simply plug the Ethernet cable into the Ethernet jack on your laptop and then connect the other end of the cable to a high-speed modem.

Modem Jack

Although most people use an Ethernet cable or a wireless signal to access the Internet, there may be times when you must use a phone line. In the event you are required to use a phone line to dial up your Internet connection, you can plug a phone cable into the modem jack to pick up a signal.

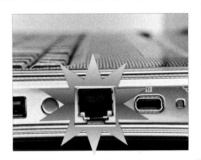

PC Card Slot

The PC card, also called the PCMCIA card (short for Personal Computer Memory Card International Association, the group of industry-leading companies that defined and develop the standard), was originally another type of storage card but ultimately expanded to house other devices such as network cards and modems. Many laptops include slots for PC cards.

Headphone and Microphone Jacks

If you want to use headphones to listen to music from your computer, you plug them into the headphone jack. Alternatively, you can use this jack to plug in computer speakers. You use the microphone jack to plug in a microphone. You might use a microphone, for example, to communicate with others using a video-chat application.

Choose a Monitor

Laptop displays range in size from 5 inches — perfect for portability — to 17 or even 20 inches. These larger monitors are ideal for handling graphics and animations. In addition to varying in size, laptop monitors can also vary in image quality.

Which monitor is right for you depends on how many hours you will spend in front of it and what functions you need to perform. When choosing a monitor, you should keep both size and image quality in mind.

Note that laptop monitors are notoriously fragile. Avoid scratching them or submitting them to extreme temperatures.

Display Size

If you mainly need to check e-mail or type a few memos on the road, a smaller monitor might be adequate. However, if you spend hours reading reports, studying graphs, and viewing high-end graphics, a larger monitor is best. Of course, monitor size affects portability, with larger monitors best suited for stay-at-home laptops.

Display Quality

Laptop monitors vary widely in quality. When researching laptop monitors, you will hear various terms, such as backlit and reflective, active matrix and passive matrix, and TFT. Generally speaking, TFT, active-matrix, backlit displays are superior. A monitor's screen resolution indicates the number of pixels that form an image on the screen; the higher the numbers are, the crisper the display. Look for a screen resolution of at least 1024 × 768 pixels — higher if you use graphics-intensive applications.

Tablet PCs

Tablet PCs are a special type of laptop. Most tablet PCs look more like legal pads than laptops. With some tablet PCs, instead of using a keyboard and pointing device to input data, you write directly on the tablet PC's monitor using a stylus — that is, an electromagnetic pen that sends a digital signal through the screen. What you write on the monitor can be converted to regular computer font for improved readability.

Choose the Right Weight

Laptops started out as portable computing devices for people who traveled regularly. Today, you can find ultraportable laptops that weigh as little as two pounds. These laptops offer a smaller display and keyboard size, but have the advantage of a longer battery life.

You can also buy laptops that weigh as much as 18 pounds. These larger models often include multimedia features and larger screen sizes. In fact, these models are so full featured, many people have adopted them for use in lieu of a desktop computer.

Choosing the right weight for your laptop involves weighing portability against performance.

Portability

If you need a laptop for use while on the road, consider a lighter-weight model. Be aware, however, that there can be a trade-off in features and price when you buy a very lightweight laptop. A two-pound laptop may be more expensive, and may be less able to handle larger programs or run at faster speeds. In contrast, a larger portable laptop may offer more speed or features, but it may be difficult to carry on long trips.

Stay-at-Home Laptops

Some people use laptops at home in lieu of a desktop model. Even larger laptops, which boast 17- or even 20-inch screens, take up less space than a computer tower, and plugging external devices into them is easier without having to crawl around on the floor or move a heavy tower. With wireless Internet connections and a built-in keyboard and pointing device, they tend to reduce the clutter of cables that come with standard desktop models. Although weight is less of an issue for stay-at-home laptops, consider whether you might want to carry such a computer from room to room or out of the house before you choose the heaviest model.

Rugged Laptops

Some laptops are marketed for their durability. If you work in an industry such as construction, the military, law enforcement, archeology, or any other industry in which your laptop may be subjected to a harsh physical environment in which heat, humidity, altitude, or depth may be a factor, one of these rugged laptops may be for you. Their keyboards are sealed to prevent water damage, and they can withstand more variation in temperature, as well as the effects of shock, vibration, drops, grease, and fire. They can also function near electromagnetic transmissions, such as from power generators. Not surprisingly, these rugged laptops are somewhat heavier than traditional models.

Determine Memory and Storage Needs

Your computer needs a certain amount of random access memory, or RAM, to run programs and load files. More RAM can also help your computer run faster. Your laptop can read from and write to RAM more quickly than to other types of computer storage.

Your computer also needs to be able to store data. You store data on a hard drive. In addition, you can store data on external storage media, such as CDs, DVDs, flash drives, and external hard drives. You will learn more about these types of external storage media in the next task.

RAM

The more random access memory (RAM) your system has, the faster items load on your computer. RAM exists on an integrated circuit memory chip, which is rated by its maximum clock rate (how quickly it can request data to appear), measured in megahertz (MHz), and its memory size, measured in megabytes (MB) or gigabytes (GB). RAM comes in several varieties, including static RAM (SRAM), dynamic RAM (DRAM), synchronous dynamic RAM (SDRAM), and double data rate SDRAM (DDR SDRAM). Note that you may be able to add RAM to your system if it is running too slowly. Doing so involves opening a panel on the bottom of the machine to access the motherboard.

Hard Drive Capacity

Hard drives have a certain capacity for storing data, measured in gigabytes (GB) or, in recent years, terabytes (TB). When you create or save a file on your laptop, the file is saved to your hard drive. You should buy a hard drive with enough capacity to handle your day-to-day data storage needs. Today, a 100GB hard drive is pretty much the minimum standard. The more files you need to store and the more programs you need to run, the larger-capacity hard drive you should get. Hard drives with a faster rotational speed can be useful for power users, enabling quicker access to files.

The Windows Experience Index

Windows 7 supports the use of the Windows Experience Index, which evaluates components on a PC, including the memory, to determine how well that PC will perform running Windows 7. This evaluation is expressed in a measurement called a *base score*. The base score is derived from the lowest of the subscores — that is, the scores of each component evaluated. Scores range from 1.0 to 7.9.

Basic Requirements

Windows 7 requires a Windows Experience Index rating of 1.0 to operate — that is, 1GB of system memory (RAM) for the 32-bit version of the operating system and 2GB of system memory (RAM) for the 64-bit version. Windows 7 also requires 20GB of available space on the hard drive to function. In reality, however, minimum requirements for operating systems are not adequate for a smooth computing experience. If you are purchasing a new laptop, you should opt for one with additional RAM and hard-drive space; how much more RAM and hard-drive space you need depends on how you plan to use your laptop.

Everyday Use

If you plan to use your laptop on a day-to-day basis, and if it fits in your budget, you should look for a PC with a Windows Experience Index rating of at least 2.0, and preferably 3.0. Bumping up your RAM to 3GB helps ensure your PC does not get bogged down. In addition, you may want to opt for a larger hard drive — say, 200GB — especially if you want to store a significant number of photos, songs, or videos on your PC.

Power Users

You may need to run several programs at once (called *multitasking*). For example, you may want to check your e-mail while running a PowerPoint presentation and opening a Word document. In this case, opt for a laptop with a Windows Experience Index rating of at least 3.0, and preferably 4.0. In addition, you may want more memory — 4GB should do the trick. And you will almost certainly want a larger hard drive.

Graphics and Gaming

For the graphics professional or hard-core gamer, a Windows Experience Index rating of at least 5.0 ensures that any high-end games or graphics applications run without a hitch. And again, you will want yet more memory and an even larger hard drive than a power user would require — 5GB of RAM and a 500GB hard drive should suffice.

Understand Drives and Data Storage

Laptops store data on an internal hard drive — a spinning hard disk inside the laptop — via magnetic recording. An arm with a magnetic head moves over the disk to read or write data on the disk as it spins. Data can also be erased, although the magnetic data pattern may remain on the drive after you have erased it.

Most laptops also have a disc drive. Depending on the type of drive, you can insert a CD, DVD, and/or Blu-ray disc into it to store data on the disc. Other data-storage options include Flash drives and portable external hard drives.

How Data Is Stored

Data is stored in files as a series of bytes in a sector on your hard drive. Each sector on the drive can contain a certain number of bytes. When you access data, whether by opening a piece of software or opening a file, the read/write heads move across the hard drive, looking for the required bytes. These bytes may be located in various sectors of the drive. Because bytes in files are spread across multiple sectors, those files are said to be *fragmented*; fragmented files take longer to load than files whose bytes are stored in a single segment.

Partitions

You can create partitions on a hard drive that essentially break it up into two or more hard drives. You may do this to run different operating systems on the same computer. You may also create a partition to foster the appearance of having multiple hard drives for file-management purposes or to accommodate multiple users. Creating additional partitions also enables you to separate your data from your operating system; that way, in the event your operating system is damaged, your data remains safe. To partition a hard drive in Windows 7, there must be either unallocated disk space or free space on the hard drive.

Using the Disc Drive

As mentioned, most laptops include a disc drive, into which you can insert various storage media. These storage media include compact discs (CDs), digital versatile discs (DVDs), and Blu-ray discs. Depending on your disc drive's setup, you may be able to read data on and write data to all three of these types of storage media.

Storing Data on CD

Nearly all disc drives support the use of compact discs, or CDs — hard plastic disks on which you can store data, music, or images. CDs can typically store up to 700MB of data. To read from or write to a CD, your laptop must have a CD drive with the appropriate support (read, write, or read/write).

Storing Data on DVD

DVDs are similar to CDs, but with more storage capacity. A single-layer DVD can store 4.7GB of data, whereas a dual-layer DVD can store twice that. DVDs come in several formats, including DVD+ , DVD−, and DVD+/−. DVDs also come in readable, writeable, and read/write format. Your laptop's disc drive must explicitly support a DVD format for you to be able to use that type of DVD.

Storing Data on Blu-ray

The name Blu-ray stems from the blue-violet laser used to read and write to this type of disc. A single-layer Blu-ray disc can store 25GB of data, more than five times the storage capacity of a standard DVD disc, and a double-layer disc can store twice that. This storage format, designed to enable the recording, playback, and rewriting of high-definition video, is expected to supersede the DVD format.

Flash Drive

A flash drive, also referred to as a USB stick or pen drive, is smaller than a pack of gum but can hold a huge amount of data. Plugging a flash drive into a USB port is like adding a second hard drive. Flash drives come with differing amounts of storage space, from 64MB to 256GB.

External Hard Drive

If you need to store large amounts of data — for example, to back up your system — you can buy an external hard drive. External hard drives have storage capacities of many gigabytes or even terabytes. An external hard drive can be connected to your laptop via its FireWire or USB port.

Select a Microprocessor

Choosing a microprocessor, often referred to as a *processor*, is an important part of deciding which laptop is right for you. The type of microprocessor found in a laptop can make a big difference in its performance.

A microprocessor incorporates most or all of the functions of a computer's central processing unit, or CPU. The microprocessor is the brain of a computer, enabling it to perform calculations and process data.

The various companies that manufacture microprocessors are constantly working to improve them. Newer microprocessors offer more processing power, handle multiple tasks concurrently, generate less heat, and require less power to operate.

What a Microprocessor Does

A microprocessor acts as the brain of the computer, handling data, performing calculations, carrying out stored instructions, and so on. Microprocessors, which are integrated circuits composed of millions of transistors, can perform many instructions per second, such as mathematical equations, calibrations, data storage, display updates, and so on. A microprocessor is housed on a tiny silicon wafer base, or chip, where some or all of the functions of a computer's central processing unit (CPU) are integrated.

Microprocessor Design

A microprocessor incorporates functions of the CPU onto an integrated circuit, also called a *chip*. An integrated circuit is a tiny electronic circuit composed of millions of transistors situated on a silicon wafer. This circuit consists mainly of semiconductor devices — that is, components that make use of the electronic properties of various semiconductor materials (primarily silicon).

Brands of Microprocessors

The two top manufacturers of microprocessors are Intel Corporation and AMD Inc. Intel, founded in 1968, produced the first microprocessor in 1971 — a four-bit processor called the Intel 4004. AMD, short for Advanced Micro Devices, launched in 1969 as a producer of logic chips. In addition to manufacturing microprocessors, both companies also produce motherboard chipsets, network interface controllers and integrated circuits, flash memory, graphic chips, and other devices for computing and communications. Chips are constantly being improved to include more processing power, handle more tasks concurrently, and generate less heat.

The x86 ISA

Both Intel and AMD produce processors based on the x86 instruction set architecture. The instruction set architecture, sometimes called simply the *instruction set* or the *ISA*, is the portion of the computer architecture that pertains to programming. It includes the *opcodes*, or the machine language that specifies the commands used by a particular processor. x86 refers to a family of ISAs spawned by the Intel 8086 chip, launched in 1978, and to the early successors of that chip, which also had names ending in 86.

Clock Rate

The higher the clock rate, the faster your computer can operate. You will often see a clock rate, also known as clock speed, expressed in gigahertz, to reflect how quickly the processor in your laptop can complete a clock cycle, or tick. A clock cycle is the smallest unit of time a device recognizes, although a microprocessor may execute several instructions in a single clock cycle. It can be useful to compare clock rates of processors in the same family; the faster the clock rate, the more instructions the microprocessor can execute per second. Using clock rates to compare processors from different families can be misleading, however, because the amount of work that different microprocessors can do in a single clock cycle varies.

Dual-Core Processors

Older laptops featured single-core processors. That is, the silicon wafer, or chip, on which the processor was housed contained only a single processor. In time, however, computer requirements exceeded the capabilities of these processors. That led to the development of dual-core processors — essentially, two processors on a single silicon wafer, or chip. Just as two heads are better than one, dual-core processors enable computers to more efficiently start and run several operations at once, at fast processing speeds (measured in GHz), and with lower power usage. Recent years have seen the development of quad-core processors, which are even more efficient than their dual-core counterparts.

Moore's Law

Moore's law, named for Intel co-founder Gordon Moore and coined in 1970 by Caltech professor Carver Mead, describes a long-term trend in computing in which the number of transistors that can be placed cheaply on an integrated circuit has roughly doubled every two years. Gordon Moore observed this trend in a 1965 paper, in which he noted that the number of components on integrated circuits had doubled each year since 1958, the year in which the integrated circuit was invented. Moore went on to posit that this trend would continue "for at least 10 years." The result of this trend, which is in fact expected to continue until at least 2015, has been the increased use and demand for digital electronic devices worldwide.

Choose a Microprocessor

The microprocessor you choose depends on how you plan to use your laptop. For example, if you are a power user or you plan to use your laptops to play games, then you will want a more robust microprocessor. In addition, if you plan to travel frequently, battery life is a consideration. In that case, you might opt for a dual-core processor designed for mobile computing, such as the AMD Turion 64 X2 or the Intel Core Duo processor. These use less power while still providing the advantages of a dual processor. Whichever microprocessor you choose, look for a clock rate of at least 1 GHz.

Review Graphics Capabilities

The graphics card is a circuit board inside your laptop that controls what appears on your laptop's monitor. The graphics card is also called the video card, video adapter, display adapter, graphics-accelerator card, or graphics processing unit. The graphics card is particularly important when playing games or running animations.

Laptops that can handle the graphics and animations that appear in many computer games tend to have powerful graphics cards along with large screens with a high resolution, a lot of memory, and fast processors. These come with a high price tag, but for a dedicated gamer or multimedia designer, they may be worth it.

Graphics Cards

Graphics cards contain a graphics processing unit (a GPU) with a specific speed and amount of memory. For most users, the graphics card that comes installed on a laptop is sufficient. For users who intend to use their laptop for graphics-rich applications such as design or animation software or games, a graphics card with more speed and memory may be required.

Considerations

If you are a hard-core gamer or plan to use your laptop to handle 3-D graphic work, a top-of-the-line graphics card is a must. However, it is not necessary to have a high-end graphics card on a laptop that will be used primarily for such tasks as checking your e-mail or using a word-processing program. Note that your graphics card must be a good match for your CPU. A very powerful graphics card with a slower or older CPU would be a waste. Also, be aware that not all graphics cards work on all computers. Finally, be sure to check the frame rate — that is, the frequency at which the card produces unique consecutive images, called *frames* — because lower rates can slow down video and animations.

Brands of Graphics Cards

Three manufacturers of graphics cards dominate the market: Intel, AMD, and NVIDIA. Intel owns the low-end category, offering a line of graphics cards integrated into the manufacturer's motherboard chipsets. Although this can reduce cost, power consumption, and noise, performance takes a hit because both the graphics card and the CPU share use of the laptop's main memory. If you plan to use your laptop primarily to check e-mail or work with a word-processing program, this type of graphics card should be adequate. If, however, you plan to use your laptop for gaming or working with 3-D graphics, an AMD and NVIDIA graphics card may be a better choice. These manufacturers offer graphics cards that span from the low end to the very high end.

Explore Wireless Capabilities

With wireless technology, you can use your laptop to connect to the Internet using a wireless network — without cable connections or a phone line. These wireless networks exist in many locations, including hotels, airports, libraries, schools, businesses, cafes, and more. If you plan to take your laptop on the road, the ability to connect to wireless networks while traveling, or at your destination, can be very important.

When you buy a laptop, you should make sure that it includes the hardware components necessary to use a wireless network. You will quickly find that a laptop without this capability is much less useful than one that has it!

How Wireless Works

A special piece of equipment called a *wireless router* broadcasts a radio-based signal, which is received by computers in the router's vicinity (assuming those computers have the appropriate hardware installed). Specifically, computers need to have a wireless card installed to access the wireless signal. Computers with the necessary hardware can use the signal for two-way communication. The transmission speed varies depending on the quality of the connection and the quality of the wireless card installed in the laptop.

Wireless Protocols

There are various wireless technology protocols. These include Bluetooth and WiFi, also referred to as 802.11. This technology enables you to connect wirelessly to the Internet. Within the WiFi protocol are several versions, including 802.11a, which operates at 54 megabits per second (Mbps) and has an indoor range of 115 feet; 802.11b, which operates at 11 Mbps but has an indoor range of 125 feet; and 802.11g, which operates at 54 Mbps with at an indoor range of 125 feet. In addition, the most recent version, 802.11n, operates at 150 Mbps with at an indoor range of 250 feet. 802.11n offers significant increases in data throughput and link range, without requiring additional bandwidth or transmission power.

Finding Wireless Networks

Many restaurants, hotels, airports, libraries, bookstores, and other public places offer wireless hot spots — that is, areas where you can use your laptop to connect to a wireless router and access the Internet for free or for a fee. In addition, you can subscribe to various wireless services from popular providers such as T-Mobile, Verizon, and so on to pick up their signal when you travel.

Choose the Best Battery

When you take your laptop on the road, it needs to carry its power supply with it — specifically, a rechargeable battery.

The amount of time you can run your laptop on a charged battery is called the *battery life*. Battery life, which varies from laptop to laptop, represents the number of hours your laptop can operate on a fully charged battery before again being recharged.

Laptop batteries come in different types. Learning about these different types before you buy can help you purchase a laptop that will serve you well for years to come.

Types of Batteries

Early laptops featured nickel-cadmium (NiCd) batteries, the first rechargeable batteries manufactured for laptops. NiCd batteries were heavy, could not hold much power, and could be recharged only a limited number of times. In addition, NiCd batteries could not be left on the charger after they had reached full charge and could not be recharged until they were completely dead. For these reasons, laptop manufacturers have since abandoned NiCd batteries. Newer laptop batteries address these issues in addition to being more efficient. These include nickel-metal hydride (NiMH) batteries and the more recent, lighter, more efficient, and more expensive lithium-ion (LiON) batteries.

Battery Life

Laptop batteries offer a certain number of hours of battery life — that is the period during which the battery is capable of operating at or above a given level after it has been fully charged. When fully charged, the average laptop battery offers anywhere from two to four hours of battery life. This number can vary, however, depending on the type of battery your laptop has, how the laptop is being used, and what types of hardware components the laptop has. Batteries with higher milliamperes per hour (MAH) have a longer battery life.

What Affects Battery Life?

Various issues affect the life of a battery. One is whether the laptop is being used or is on standby mode. Another is how long the laptop takes to power down or power up. In addition, having a larger monitor with higher resolution or one used at a higher brightness setting can drain a battery faster. And of course, battery life depends on the type of battery you have. Fortunately, laptop PCs have several tools for prolonging battery life, from dimming the screen display to automatically switching to a standby mode when not in use for a prescribed period of time.

Sleep Mode

One way to stretch your battery life is to put your laptop into Sleep mode when you are not using it. Sleep mode turns off the screen, hard drive, and internal fan, and generally uses less energy. When your laptop comes out of Sleep mode, whatever you were doing when the laptop went into Sleep mode is still open and available for you to return to work. In addition to using Sleep mode, you can use Hibernate mode. In Hibernate mode, the laptop is completely powered down; when you restart the laptop, whatever you were doing when the laptop went into Hibernate mode again appears on the Windows 7 desktop.

Gauging Your Charge

Your laptop keeps you informed of your battery charge in a couple of ways. First, the Windows 7 taskbar displays a battery meter that shows you how much charge you have left. You can also set a low-battery alarm to alert you when power is just about to run out. To learn how to set a low-battery alarm, see Chapter 2.

Charging Your Battery

You will need to charge your laptop battery on a regular basis. You do this by plugging your laptop's power cord into an electrical outlet. Getting in the habit of keeping your battery charged is essential. Unless your laptop has an older battery that requires you to wait until the battery is practically drained to recharge it, your motto should be, "Charge often!"

Run on AC Power

If you are using your laptop at your home or office, you can plug its power adapter into an electrical outlet and run off of electricity all the time. This has the added benefit of recharging your battery and keeping it fully charged. If you lose your adapter, damage it, or it simply stops working, you can buy a replacement. Note, though, that you must find an adapter designed to work with your make and model of laptop.

Add a Second Battery

The easiest way to stretch the time you have to work on your laptop with a battery is to double your battery power by carrying a spare. When the first one runs low, simply swap them out, inserting your spare battery to keep using your laptop. Some laptops are designed with quick-swapping in mind, enabling you to simply eject the spent battery and quickly insert the spare, without even shutting down your system. Other laptops require that you power down your computer first. Note that the spare battery must fit your laptop model; be sure to get the right model battery, or it will not work.

Battery Life Expectancy

Different types of batteries have different life expectancies. Although lithium-ion batteries have the longest life spans — about 500 charges — even they eventually wear down. As batteries wear down, they are no longer able to hold a charge for as long as when they were new, or they may fail to fully charge. If you find yourself in need of a new battery, contact your laptop's manufacturer to purchase one. When purchasing a new battery, beware of generics. Always buy a manufacturer, or manufacturer approved battery. Be aware that new batteries can be quite expensive.

Chapter 2

Setting Up Your Laptop PC

When you bring home a new laptop, you will want to take some time to explore how its various components, such as the pointing device and keyboard, operate.

In addition, you will want to set up your laptop so that you can use it as efficiently as possible right out of the gate. This might involve connecting a printer, microphone, or other hardware device; changing screen settings; selecting a power plan to maximize battery life; and more.

And of course, you will need to master the basics of starting your laptop, getting help, and shutting it down.

Turn the Laptop On

You should take a moment to get used to how your laptop computer opens and powers on. Although laptop models vary slightly in how the latch on the laptop case operates, most work in a similar fashion.

When you power on your laptop, Windows 7 displays a Welcome screen. If multiple user accounts are set up on your laptop, you are prompted to select the user account you want to use. Depending on that account's settings, you may also be prompted to enter a password. (You will learn how to password-protect your laptop in Chapter 13.)

Turn the Laptop On

1 Open the laptop.

2 Press the Power button.

In a few moments, the computer boots up, and your operating system's Welcome screen appears.

Charge the Battery

If you are using your laptop at your home or office, you can power it by plugging it into an electrical outlet. If, however, you are on the road, you can run your laptop on battery power. Most laptop batteries can run for two to four hours, depending on the laptop's setup.

When the battery runs down, you can recharge it by plugging your laptop back into an electrical outlet using the cord that came with it. (The time it takes for a laptop battery to recharge varies; consult your user manual for details.) Keeping your battery charged is essential.

Charge the Battery

① Plug the power cord into the appropriate slot on your laptop.

② Plug the other end of the power cord into an electrical outlet.

Note: *If you travel globally, find out what type of electric adapter you will need in your destination country. Without such an adapter, you could seriously damage your laptop if you attempt to plug it into a wall outlet to charge the battery.*

The power icon in the notification area of the taskbar changes from ▯ to ▯.

Use a Touchpad

Your laptop's built-in pointing device can deliver full mouse functionality, enabling you to move the mouse pointer as needed and click to make selections, choose commands, and perform other important tasks.

The most common type of laptop pointing device is a touchpad. A touchpad, sometimes called a trackpad, is a flat surface that detects finger contact; you move your finger to move the mouse pointer on-screen.

Laptops featuring this type of pointing device typically also feature two large buttons, usually somewhere beneath the touchpad. You can press these buttons to perform traditional left- and right-mouse button functions such as making a selection (left) or revealing a context menu (right).

Use a Touchpad

1 Place your finger on the touchpad.

Note the position of the mouse pointer on your monitor.

2 Slide your finger around the touchpad.

Note how the mouse pointer moves on the screen.

3 Press the left button.

The action that occurs depends on the location of the mouse pointer when you pressed the button. For example, if the mouse pointer was over the Start button when you clicked, the Windows 7 Start menu opens.

4 Press the right button.

A context menu appears.

Explore a Wireless Mouse

Many people have difficulty getting used to a touchpad or other pointing device on their laptops. If you find a traditional mouse easier to use, you can purchase a wireless mouse.

A wireless mouse is a natural addition to any laptop. It does not require cables, it is lightweight, and it replaces the sometimes awkward touchpad or other pointing device on

your laptop with the familiar functionality of the desktop mouse.

Several wireless mice are on the market, including ones made especially for laptops. These are smaller than desktop mice, making them easy to bring with you when you travel with your laptop.

The Elements of a Mouse

Mice come in different styles, but most include a right and left button and a scroll wheel. The left button is used for clicking in a file, to position your cursor, and for clicking and dragging to select objects and text. The right button is used to display shortcut menus. You can roll the scroll wheel to scroll through windows.

How a Wireless Mouse Works

When you purchase a wireless mouse, you also receive a transmitter that plugs into your laptop's USB port. When you plug in the transmitter, Windows 7 typically detects it and installs the necessary software, called a *driver*, for the transmitter and mouse to work. The wireless mouse then overrides the built-in mouse function.

Choose the Mouse

You can find a wireless mouse specifically designed for laptop users. They are smaller than a traditional mouse, and easily fit in a small space such as a pocket of a laptop bag. Higher priced versions of wireless mice may feature an extended range and greater precision.

Get to Know the Keyboard

One of the most important features of a laptop is how its keyboard feels to you. Laptop keyboards can vary from those condensed for space — depending on function keys to provide full functionality — to expansive, desktop-style keyboards with number pads and special shortcut keys. Your choice of keyboard is most directly related to the size and weight of laptop that you need.

In addition to the alphanumeric keys that you press to enter text, laptops often include specialized keys. For example, the Windows key (⊞) is used to open the Windows Start menu on a laptop running Windows. Other special keys are discussed here.

Modifying Keys

Several keys on your keyboard are used to modify actions. For instance, **Shift**, **Ctrl**, and **Alt**, when pressed with another key, modify how that key works. As an example, pressing **Ctrl** + **C** copies the selected text or object in a file, and pressing **Ctrl** + **V** pastes the copied text or object. These combinations of keys are called *keyboard shortcuts*. And of course, pressing **Shift** plus any letter capitalizes the letter. Note that you can also use many of these keys in conjunction with clicking your mouse or pointing device to perform certain actions. For example, pressing **Ctrl** while clicking files in a folder window enables you to select multiple files.

Navigation Keys

If, like many users, you find it difficult to maneuver with the pointing device built into your laptop, you should consider adopting the use of the various navigation keys to move your cursor around: **End**, **Home**, **Pgup**, **Pgdn**, ⬇, ⬆, ⬅, and ➡. Pressing **End** moves the cursor to the end of the current line. Pressing **Home** moves the cursor to the beginning of the current line. Pressing **Pgup** or **Pgdn** moves the cursor up one page or down one page, respectively. And pressing the directional keys ⬇, ⬆, ⬅, and ➡ moves the cursor down, up, left, and right.

Function Keys

Function keys are available on all laptop keyboards to provide shortcuts to functions in programs. Function keys marked **F1** to **F12** initiate different actions, depending on the program in which you are working. For example, pressing **F1** while working in Microsoft WordPad opens a Windows Help and Support window with links to help articles about WordPad. On a laptop, where space is at a premium, there is often a key labeled **Fn**; by pressing this key along with a function key, you can initiate a different function than you would by pressing the function key alone. For example, on the author's laptop, pressing **Fn** at the same time as **F1** locks the laptop.

Escape Key

Pressing `Esc` stops a current action. In Windows, this key acts as a shortcut for clicking a No button, Quit button, Exit button, Cancel button, or Abort button, making it useful if you want to back out of an action or leave a dialog box or other input screen without saving an entry. Pressing `Esc` is also a common shortcut for clicking the Stop button found in many Web browsers, as well as a shortcut for pausing games or displaying a game's menu. This key is typically located in the upper-left corner of your keyboard, to the left of the function keys.

Caps Lock Key

Pressing Caps Lock toggles the Caps Lock feature on and off. With Caps Lock on, anything you type appears in uppercase. With Caps Lock off, everything you type is lowercase, and you need to press `Shift` to capitalize a letter, such as the first letter of the first word in a sentence, the first letter in a person's name, or the word "I." On many keyboards, a small light becomes illuminated when the Caps Lock feature has been toggled on. Note that toggling on the Caps Lock feature does not affect nonletter keys, such as number keys or punctuation keys.

Keys for Cursor Placement

`Enter` is used to start a new paragraph in a text document, or to accept an entry in a dialog box. `Spacebar` is used to add a space between letters in a sentence. Press `Del` to delete a selected object or text. Press `Backspace` to move your cursor back one character or space. Press `Insert` to switch from Overtype mode to Insert mode. In Overtype mode, text you type overwrites existing text to the right of the cursor; in Insert mode, existing text to the right of the cursor is moved to the right when you add new text. Press `Tab` to advance the cursor to the next tab stop or to move to the next field in a dialog box.

The Embedded Numeric Keypad

All keyboards feature a row of number keys along the top. The placement of these keys, however, makes entering a lot of numbers difficult. For this reason, most keyboards include a numeric keypad, which is laid out similarly to a calculator, to speed number entry. On most desktop keyboards, this numeric keypad is on the far right. On laptops, where space is limited, the calculator-style numeric keypad is embedded within the letter and number keys on the rightmost side of the keyboard. When you turn on the Num Lock feature by pressing Num Lock or the appropriate function-key combination, those keys turn into numeric-keypad keys.

Connect a Printer or Hardware Device

With Windows 7, connecting printers, scanners, Web cams, and other hardware to your laptop is a snap. In fact, in most cases, after you connect the device to your laptop via the appropriate port, Windows 7 locates the software it needs to interact with the device (called a *driver*) online and installs it with no input from you.

If Windows 7 is unable to install a driver, it generally notifies you and offers suggestions on what steps to take next. In the event Windows 7 fails to do this, you can start a wizard to set up any hardware you connect.

Connect a Printer or Hardware Device

Start the Add a Device Wizard

1. Click the **Start** button (🔵).
2. Click **Devices and Printers**.

The Devices and Printers window opens.

3. Click **Add a device**.

Windows 7 launches the Add a Device Wizard.

Note: *Simply disconnect the device from your laptop to remove it.*

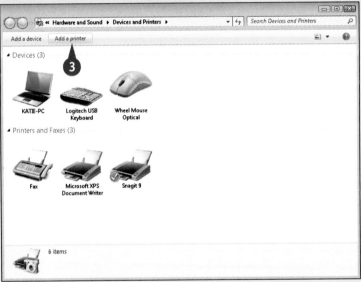

Start the Add a Printer Wizard

1 Click the **Start** button (⊞).

2 Click **Devices and Printers**.

The Devices and Printers window opens.

3 Click **Add a printer**.

Windows 7 launches the Add a Printer Wizard.

What do you do if the wizard fails to set up your hardware?
In most cases, Windows 7 installs the necessary drivers for your hardware automatically when you connect a printer or other device to your laptop. If it fails to do so, and if stepping through the Add a Device or Add a Printer Wizard does not resolve the problem, you may need to obtain the necessary drivers from the manufacturer of your device. The easiest way to do this is to visit the manufacturer's Web site and download the driver. Alternatively, if the device came with a CD or DVD, that disc likely contains the necessary drivers to run the device with your laptop.

Connect and Test a Microphone

If you plan to record sound files, such as narrations for PowerPoint presentations, you need a microphone. You can also use a microphone to take advantage of the Speech Recognition features in Windows 7. Finally, you need a microphone if you intend to use your laptop to communicate with others using VoIP services such as Skype or MSN.

The first time you connect your microphone to your laptop, you should take a few moments to set it up to make sure that it picks up your voice clearly. To help you with this, Windows 7 includes the Microphone Setup Wizard.

Connect and Test a Microphone

1 After plugging your microphone or headset into the appropriate port on your laptop, click the **Start** button (⊞).

2 In the Start menu's Search field, type **microphone**.

Windows displays a list of items that match what you typed.

3 Click **Set up a microphone**.

The first screen of the Microphone Setup Wizard opens.

4 Click the option button (⊙) next to the type of microphone you want to set up (here, **Headset Microphone**).

5 Click **Next**.

6 Click **Next** again to skip the next screen in the wizard.

⑦ With the microphone situated near your mouth, read the sample sentence.

⑧ Click **Next**.

Note: If the wizard informs you that it could not hear your speech, check the connection of your microphone to your laptop and ensure that the microphone's Mute button has not been engaged. Then read the sentence again.

Windows sets up your microphone.

⑨ Click **Finish**.

How do you set up headphones?
Although most laptops have built-in speakers, when you travel with a laptop, headphones can be a great way to cut down on sound around you. In addition, if you want to listen to audio CDs or other types of sound files, headphones keep your listening experience private. Headphones come in several types, from clip-on, earbud, and ear-canal headphones to earpad-style headphones that fit over your ear to full-size headphones that cover your ears completely. Setting up headphones is a simple matter of plugging them into your laptop's headphone jack. (For help identifying a headphone jack, refer to Chapter 1.)

Change the Screen Resolution

You can change your laptop PC's screen resolution. With a higher screen resolution, text and images on your screen appear sharper. In addition, they are smaller, meaning that more items fit on the screen. With a lower screen resolution, items on your screen may appear less crisp, but they will be larger, and therefore easier to see. Items on a screen with a resolution of 800 × 600 appear much larger than in a screen with a resolution of, say, 1280 × 800.

How you set your screen resolution is largely a matter of personal taste, but larger monitors do often require a higher screen resolution.

Change the Screen Resolution

① Right-click a blank area of the desktop.

② Click **Screen resolution**.

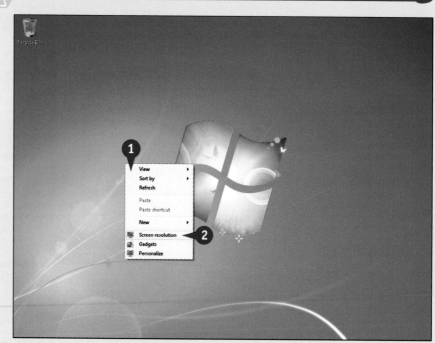

The Screen Resolution window appears.

③ Click the **Resolution** ▾.

④ Drag the **Resolution** slider to the desired resolution.

⑤ Click **OK**.

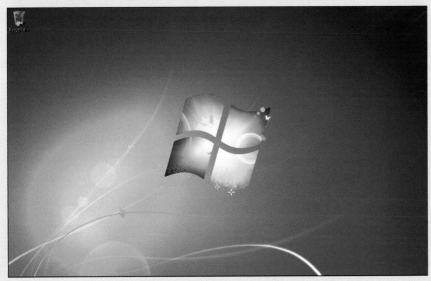

Windows prompts you to confirm the change.

⑥ Click **Keep changes**.

Windows changes the screen resolution.

Can I add a second monitor to my laptop?
If your laptop features a monitor port, it should support the addition of an external monitor. If so, you add an external monitor by following these steps:

① Power down your laptop.

② Connect the monitor to your laptop using a standard monitor cable.

③ Plug the monitor into an electrical power source.

④ Turn on the monitor.

⑤ Restart your laptop.

Windows 7 should detect the monitor and install any necessary drivers.

Change the Desktop Background

Your laptop features a default desktop background — most likely one that features a Windows 7 logo or a design supplied by the computer manufacturer.

If you do not like the desktop background that appears by default, you can choose a different image or set of images. One option is to select from the Windows 7 predesigned backgrounds; alternatively, you can choose from your own photos. A third option is to obtain images online to use for your desktop background.

In addition, you can set a screen saver, which appears when your system is idle for a prescribed period of time.

Change the Desktop Background

1 Right-click a blank area of the desktop.

2 Click **Personalize**.

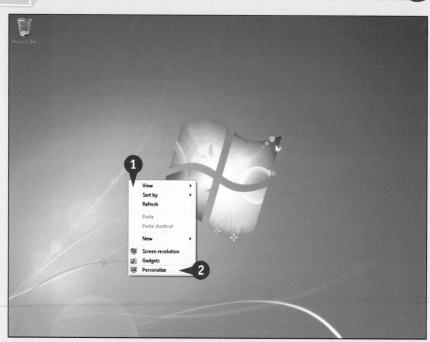

The Personalization window appears.

3 Click **Desktop Background**.

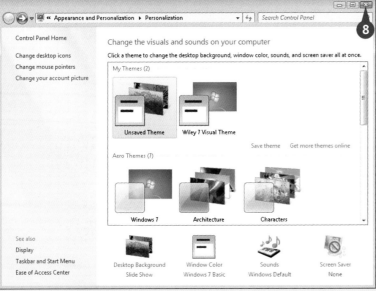

The Choose Your Desktop Background window opens.

④ Click the **Picture location** ⊡ and select **Windows Desktop Backgrounds**.

● To choose from your own images, click **Browse,** locate your photo folder, and then click **OK**.

⑤ Position the mouse pointer over the image you want to use as the desktop background and then click the check box (☑) that appears.

⑥ Click the **Picture position** ⊡ and select how the image(s) should appear on-screen.

● If you have selected multiple images, click the **Change picture every** ⊡ and select how often the pictures should change.

● To display multiple images in random order, select the **Shuffle** option.

⑦ Click **Save changes**.

Windows changes the desktop background.

⑧ Click the **Close** button (☒) to close the Personalization window.

Simplify It

How do you set a screen saver?
Setting a screen saver — that is, a still or animated picture that appears on your laptop's screen when the pointing device and keyboard have been inactive for a prescribed period of time — prevents others from viewing your desktop when you are away from your laptop. To turn off the screen saver and again view the Windows desktop, simply use your pointing device or press a key on your keyboard. You choose a screen saver from the Screen Saver Settings dialog box; to open it, right-click a blank area of the desktop, click **Personalize**, and click **Screen Saver** in the Personalization window.

View Mobility Settings

Windows 7 includes many laptop-specific settings. As you might guess, many of these settings relate to conserving power — something especially critical when you must use a battery to power your PC. For example, you can reduce the brightness of the laptop display to minimize power usage. Other settings pertain to connecting to the Internet via wireless access points, synchronizing your laptop with another PC, and giving presentations.

To make it easy to access all these laptop-specific settings, Windows 7 has a special window called Windows Mobility Center. You access this window through the Windows 7 Control Panel.

View Mobility Settings

① Click **Start** (⊞).

② Click **Control Panel**.

The Control Panel window appears.

③ Click **Hardware and Sound**.

The Hardware and Sound window appears.

4 Click **Windows Mobility Center**.

The Windows Mobility Center window appears.

Note: *An even faster way to open the Windows Mobility Center window is to right-click the power icon (▣) in the taskbar's notification area and select Windows Mobility Center from the menu that appears.*

How do you adjust display settings?
You can set up your laptop to conserve power by adjusting the brightness of the display. Alternatively, you might adjust the display brightness to ease eyestrain or generally make your screen easier to see. To adjust the brightness, drag the **Brightness** slider in the Windows Mobility Center to the left to make the screen more dim or drag the slider to the right to brighten the screen. For additional brightness settings, click the **Change Display Brightness** button (▣). The screen that appears enables you to specify under what circumstances the display should be dimmed, turned off, and put to sleep.

Choose a Power Plan

Windows 7 offers three power plans for laptop computers: Power Saver, High Performance, and Balanced.

Use Power Saver when the laptop is running on battery. It shuts down various components after the system has been idle for a short period of time to conserve power.

Use High Performance when the laptop is plugged in. It waits longer to shut down components when the system is idle.

Use Balanced, the default, if you do not want to bother changing plans when your power supply changes. It offers a happy medium between Power Saver and High Performance. Note that you can modify plans as needed.

Choose a Power Plan

Choose a Different Power Plan

1. In the Windows Mobility Center window, click the **Battery Status** ⏷.

2. Click a different plan.

   Windows applies the plan you chose.

Modify a Power Plan

1. In the Windows Mobility Center window, click the **Change Power Settings** button (▥).

The Power Options window appears.

Note: *A faster way to open the Power Options window is to right-click the power icon (*🔋*) in the taskbar's notification area and select* **Power Options** *from the menu that appears.*

2 Click **Change plan settings** for the power plan you want to change.

The Edit Plan Settings page appears.

3 Click the ▾ to adjust the On Battery options.

4 Click and drag the slider to set the Adjust Plan Brightness setting under the On Battery option.

5 Click the ▾ to adjust the Plugged In options.

6 Click and drag the slider to set the Adjust Plan Brightness setting under the Plugged In option.

For more options, click **Change advanced power settings**.

7 Click **Save changes**.

How do you set a low-battery alarm?
To set up Windows 7 to alert you when your laptop's battery levels are low, open the Edit Plan Settings window for your power plan. Then click **Change advanced power settings**. Click the plus button (⊞) to the left of **Battery** entry. Click the plus button (⊞) to the left of the **Low battery notification** subentry. Click **On battery** to reveal a ▾, click the ▾, and click **On**. Click **OK**. Click **Save changes**.

Get Help

Suppose you run into a problem with Windows 7 or you are not sure how to perform a task — for example, you want to find out how to create a user account. The Windows Help and Support Center is your first stop for expert assistance. Using the Windows Help and Support Center, you can search for help by entering a keyword or phrase, such as user account. When you do, the Windows Help and Support Center displays a list of links to related help articles. If your computer is connected to the Internet, the list even includes links to online resources.

Get Help

1 Click the **Start** button (🔲).

2 Click **Help and Support**.

The Windows Help and Support window appears.

3 Type a keyword or phrase in the **Search** box.

4 Click the **Search Help** button (🔍) or press Enter.

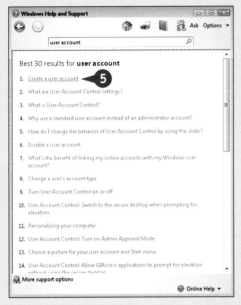

Windows displays a list of links to help articles that relate to the word or phrase you typed.

⑤ Click a link that looks relevant.

Windows displays the article.

Note: *The Help and Support Center cannot help you with a program that is not included with the Windows 7 operating system, such as Microsoft Excel or Adobe Photoshop. To access help in these programs, click the* **Help** *menu or the* **Help** *icon (⬛) in the program window.*

Simplify It

Can you get help via Remote Assistance?
Yes. Another way to resolve a computer problem is to invite someone you trust to help you via Remote Assistance — regardless of his or her physical location. During a Remote Assistance session, you and your helper can communicate via chat. In addition, your helper can view your computer screen and, with your permission, use his or her mouse and keyboard to make changes to your system. To start a Remote Assistance session, you can use the Windows Remote Assistance Wizard. You launch the wizard by clicking the **Start** button (⬛), clicking **All Programs**, clicking the **Maintenance** folder, and clicking **Windows Remote Assistance**.

Shut Down Your Laptop

When you are finished using your laptop, you should shut it down. Shutting down your laptop when you are not using it is important for conserving energy.

Although you might be tempted to simply press the power button to shut down your laptop, you should not. Windows requires that you perform a specific set of steps to shut down your laptop to ensure that you do not lose important data by accident.

In addition to shutting down your laptop, you can choose other options, such as Sleep and Hibernate. You will learn about these and other options in this task.

Shut Down Your Laptop

1. Click **Start** (⊞).

2. To shut down your PC, click **Shut down**. Windows shuts down the computer.

3. Alternatively, point to the right arrow (▷) next to the **Shut down** option.

Windows displays additional choices.

● Click **Sleep** to place your laptop in stand-by mode, in which power is withheld from nonessential components and operations. When a sleeping system is awakened, it resumes operation quickly.

● Click **Hibernate** to save your data and power down your computer, but keep your desktop intact. When you restart the system, it reverts to the state it was in before it entered hibernation — with all the same programs, folders, and files displayed on the desktop.

● Click **Switch user** to switch to a different user account without closing the programs open in the current account.

● Click **Log off** to close all open programs and log off of your account. This returns Windows to the Welcome screen.

● Click **Lock** to lock the computer. To unlock the computer, enter the password specified for the current user account (assuming one has been set).

● Click **Restart** to close all open programs, shut down Windows, and then start Windows back up again. You might choose this option if, for example, you installed new software that requires restarting Windows before it can be used.

④ Close your laptop by pushing the lid down.

How do you change default power options?

❶ Right-click the power icon (▣) in the taskbar and select **Power Options**.

❷ In the left panel of the Power Options window, click **Choose What Power Buttons Do**.

❸ Click the **When I Press the Power Button** ▾ under On Battery and choose Do Nothing, Sleep, Hibernate, or Shut Down.

❹ Repeat Step **3** under Plugged In.

❺ Repeat Steps **3** and **4** for the When I Close the Lid setting.

❻ Click **Save changes**.

Chapter 3

Using Software Programs on Your Laptop PC

Laptop PCs running Windows 7 come bundled with several preinstalled programs, also referred to as applications. These preinstalled programs include WordPad, a full-featured word-processing application; Paint, used to create drawings and otherwise edit digital images; various games; a calculator; and more.

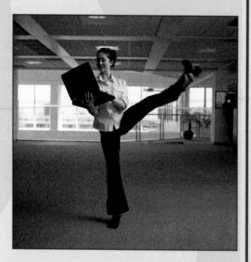

In addition to these are countless other Windows 7-compatible programs. Some, like the downloadable programs offered on Microsoft's Windows Live Web site, are available free of charge; others are available for purchase.

Although not all programs operate in exactly the same way, many do share common tools and features, as outlined in this chapter.

Get to Know the Windows Desktop

The Windows 7 desktop serves as the starting point for any task you want to perform using your laptop. For example, from the Windows 7 desktop you access the Start menu, from which you can launch programs, access files, and locate settings for Windows 7.

The Windows 7 desktop also enables you to keep track of what programs you have running, switch among those programs, and close them as needed. The desktop also displays important information about your computer's operation.

Familiarizing yourself with the various components of the Windows 7 desktop is critical.

Start Button

Click the **Start** button (⊞) to reveal the Start menu. This menu offers access to available programs, the Windows Help and Support area, the Control Panel, and more.

Desktop Shortcuts

Double-click a shortcut icon to a program or file to launch it. To create a shortcut, right-click the item in the Start menu or Windows Explorer, click **Send To**, and then click **Desktop (Create Shortcut)**.

Taskbar

The taskbar displays icons for all programs you have open. By default, the taskbar features icons for launching Internet Explorer 8, Windows Explorer, and Windows Media Player.

Notification Area

This area displays information about your computer, such as whether it is connected to a wireless network. It also displays alert icons if your system is in need of attention.

Show Desktop Button

Click the **Show Desktop** button to minimize any open windows and reveal the desktop.

Work Area

Windows 7 displays any programs, folders, and files that you open in the work area.

Start a Program

Before you can begin working with an application, also called a program, you must instruct Windows 7 to launch it. When you do, Windows 7 starts the program and opens its program window on the desktop.

You can launch an application in a few ways. One is to use the Start menu, as described here.

Another is to double-click the program's shortcut icon on the desktop (assuming one exists). Some programs — namely, Internet Explorer, Windows Explorer, and Windows Media Player — can be launched from the Windows 7 taskbar. Alternatively, you can open a file associated with that program in Windows Explorer.

Start a Program

1 Click **Start** (⊞).

● If the program you want to start appears in the first pane of the Start menu, click it to launch it.

2 Click **All Programs**. The All Programs menu option changes to a Back menu option.

3 If necessary, click the subfolder containing the program you want to run.

4 Click the program you want to start.

The program you selected opens in a window on the desktop, and a button for the program appears in the taskbar.

Note: *A faster way to start a program is to type its name in the Search bar at the bottom of the Start menu. As you type, Windows displays a list of programs that match your text; click the program in the list to start it.*

Navigate Program Windows

When you start a program, its program window appears on the Windows desktop. Although not all program windows are the same, many share certain navigation elements in common. Taking time to familiarize yourself with these elements makes navigating program windows much easier.

These elements include the Window Menu button, the Quick Access toolbar, the title bar, various buttons for resizing and closing the program window, scroll bars, a work area, and more. In addition, many programs feature what Microsoft calls the *Ribbon*, which offers an intuitive way to locate and execute commands; other programs have retained traditional pull-down menus and toolbars.

Title Bar

The program window's title bar displays the name of the program as well as the name of the file open in the program window.

Window Menu Button

Clicking the Window Menu button reveals commands for restoring, moving, sizing, minimizing, maximizing, and closing the program window. (Note that the appearance of this button differs by program.)

Program Window Controls

Use these buttons to minimize the program window, resize the window, or close the window.

Work Area

The work area is where files you have opened in the program appear. It is where you add and work with data in a program.

File Tab

Click the File tab to access options for creating a new file, opening an existing file, saving a file, printing a file, and more.

Ribbon

Some programs feature a Ribbon instead of traditional pull-down menus and toolbars. The Ribbon displays groups of related commands in tabs.

Quick Access Toolbar

You can use the buttons on this toolbar to launch the Save, Undo, or Redo command. Note that you can change which buttons appear here.

Scroll Bars

If your file cannot be viewed in its entirety in the work area, drag the vertical and horizontal scroll bars to scroll through the data in the file.

Status Bar

The status bar displays information about the file currently open in the program window.

Zoom Controls

Use the Zoom In and Zoom Out buttons or the Zoom slider to zoom your view of the file open in the program window.

Resize and Move Program Windows

Often, you may need to move or resize a program window you have open on your Windows 7 desktop. For example, you might need to make a program window smaller or move a program window in order to view other programs you have running on your laptop or to access an item on your desktop such as a shortcut icon.

In addition to resizing and moving a program window, you can minimize it. When you minimize a program window, you remove it from the desktop; when you are ready to view it again, simply click its button on the taskbar.

Resize and Move Program Windows

Resize a Program Window

1 To reduce the size of a window that covers the entire screen, click **Restore Down** button (⬜).

● The program window shrinks to a predefined size.

● The Restore Down button (⬜) changes to a Maximize button (⬜).

*Note: To maximize the program window so it again covers the entire screen, click the **Maximize** button (⬜).*

Move a Program Window

1 Click an empty section of the program window's title bar.

2 Drag the window in the direction you want it to move.

3 When the window is in the desired location, release the mouse button.

Can you resize a window manually?
Yes. Resizing a window manually enables you to fine-tune its dimensions. Position your mouse pointer over the edge of the window border you want to move. When the pointer changes to a two-headed arrow, click and drag it inward or outward to resize the window, and then release the mouse button.

How do you minimize a window?
To minimize a window, click the **Minimize** button ( ). The program window disappears, but its taskbar button remains in place. To restore the window to its original size and location, simply click its taskbar button. Alternatively, close a window by clicking its **Close** button ( ). The program window and its taskbar button disappear.

Work with Multiple Program Windows

Many laptop users multitask, running more than one program at a time or launching multiple files in a single program. Multitasking, though certainly an efficient way to work, can make navigating your Windows system difficult.

Fortunately, Windows 7 includes several tools for switching among multiple open program windows, including taskbar buttons and keyboard commands. Windows 7 also makes it easy to focus your attention on whatever program window is most important, using its Shake feature. And regardless of how many program windows you have open, you can access the desktop with a single click of a button.

Work with Multiple Program Windows

Switch Program Windows

1 Click the taskbar button for the program window to which you want to switch.

● Windows 7 displays in the work area the program window whose button you clicked.

Note: *Another way to switch program windows is to press* Alt *+* Tab. *Windows displays thumbnail images of each window currently open on your laptop; continue pressing* Alt *+* Tab *until the thumbnail for the window to which you want to switch is highlighted. Alternatively, press* Alt *+* Esc *to simply switch to the next window in the cycle.*

Shake to Minimize Extra Windows

1 Click the title bar of the window you want to remain visible and, holding down the mouse button, move the mouse pointer back and forth to shake it.

● Windows minimizes all the open windows except the one you shook.

Note: *You can redisplay the minimized windows by shaking the visible window a second time.*

Simplify It

How do you switch among multiple windows running the same program?
To switch to a different window running the same program, position your mouse pointer over the program's taskbar button and, in the list of open windows that appears, click the window to which you want to switch. Alternatively, press and hold Ctrl and click the program's taskbar button to cycle through the open windows.

Can you display two windows side by side?
Yes. Click the title bar of either window, drag it to the left edge of the screen, and release the mouse button. The window snaps into place, filling the left half of the work area. Repeat for the remaining window, dragging it to the right.

Explore the Ribbon

Instead of the menus and toolbars found in many older programs, several Windows 7 applications feature the Ribbon, which offers an intuitive way to locate and execute commands.

The Ribbon is grouped into tabs, each containing sections of related commands. For example, the Home tab in Microsoft WordPad contains commands for changing the font, setting text alignment, indenting text, and so on. Some tabs appear only when needed, such as when you are working with a table or picture in a file.

The Ribbon is maximized by default, but you can minimize it to view more of your program window.

Explore the Ribbon

Use the Ribbon

① Click a tab.

The tab organizes related tasks and commands into logical groups.

② Click a button to activate a command or feature.

● Clicking a button with arrows displays additional commands.

Minimize the Ribbon

1 Double-click a tab name.

● The Ribbon is minimized.

2 Double-click the tab name again to maximize the Ribbon.

Note: *To use a Ribbon while it is minimized, simply click the tab containing the tools that you want to access to reveal it.*

How do you use menus and toolbars?
Traditional pull-down menus and toolbars do still exist in certain programs. To use a pull-down menu, click the name of the menu you want to display; then click the command you want to run or the feature you want to enable or disable. (You may need to click a submenu to access the desired command or feature.) To use a toolbar, click the button that represents the command you want to run or the feature you want to enable or disable. In some cases, clicking an item in a toolbar reveals a drop-down list with additional options; simply click the desired option in the list.

Use Dialog Boxes

Often, if a program needs you to supply information, it displays a dialog box. For example, when you save a document for the first time, Windows displays the Save As dialog box; here you can indicate the folder in which you want to save the file, the name you want to give the file, and so on.

Dialog boxes feature various types of input controls to enable you to supply information to the program, including drop-down lists, option buttons, spin boxes, check boxes, and text boxes.

Many dialog boxes contain a Help button; click it to find out more about the various settings.

List Box

A list box displays a list of options; you simply click the item you want to select. Scroll bars enable you to move through a longer list to see all available options.

Option Button

You click an option button to enable (⦿) or disable (◯) the feature associated with it. Only one option button in a group can be enabled at once.

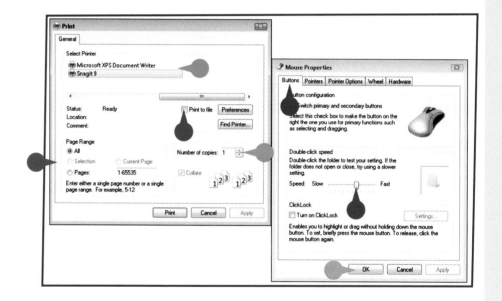

Check Box

Clicking a check box enables (☑) or disables (☐) the feature associated with it. Unlike an option button, multiple check boxes in a group can be enabled at once.

Spin Box

You can click the up and down arrows on a spin box (⬍) to increase or decrease the value in the box, respectively. You can also simply type a value in the text box.

Tab

Some dialog boxes have tabs along the top, each displaying a different set of controls. To switch tabs, simply click the desired tab.

Slider Control

A slider control enables you to made incremental adjustments to a setting.

Command Button

You click a command button to execute the command described on the button — for example, Cancel to close a dialog box without applying your changes.

Text Box

You type text in a text box. For example, you might enter a page range to print in the Print dialog box or the name you want to apply to a file in the Save As dialog box.

Drop-Down List Box

A drop-down list box looks somewhat like a text box, but with a down-arrow button (▾) on the side. To change the setting, click the button and select a different option from the list that appears.

Keyboard Shortcuts for Navigating Dialog Boxes	
Keyboard Shortcut	**Associated Action**
Enter	Select the default command button (indicated by a highlight).
Esc	Close the dialog box without implementing your changes. (Pressing Esc is the same as clicking the Cancel command button.)
Tab	Move forward through the controls in the dialog box.
Shift + Tab	Move backward through the dialog box controls.
↑/↓	Move up or down within a group of option buttons.
Alt + ↓	Reveal the available options in the selected drop-down list box.

Create and Save a File

To work with data in a Windows 7 program on your laptop, you must create a new file in which to store it.

If you want to be able to refer to the data in the file at some later time, you must save the file. You should also frequently save any file you are working on in case of a power failure or computer crash.

When you save a file, you can give it a unique filename, set the file type, and store it in any folder you choose. You can then open the saved file at a later time.

Create and Save a File

Create a File

1 Click the **File** tab.

2 Click **New**.

> **Note:** *Some programs require you to provide additional information when creating a new file. For example, if you are creating a new document in Microsoft Word, you are prompted to indicate what type of document you want to create.*

● The new file opens.

> **Note:** *An even faster way to create a new file is to press* Ctrl + N.

Save a File

1 Click the **File** tab.

● For subsequent saves, you can click the **Save** button (⊞) on the Quick Access toolbar to quickly save the file, or press `Ctrl` + `S`.

2 Position your mouse pointer over the **Save as** option.

3 If prompted, click a file type.

The Save As dialog box appears.

4 In the Navigation pane, click the library in which you want to save the file.

5 In the subfolder list, click the folder in which you want to save the file, for example Documents.

6 Type a name for the file in the **File name** field.

7 Click **Save**.

The program saves the file and the new filename appears on the window's title bar.

Simplify It

What if you want to save a new version of a file but leave the original version intact?
Suppose you are tweaking a form letter that you send out to clients but you want to keep a copy of the original for your records. To do so, launch the Save As dialog box and specify the library and folder in which you want to save the new version of the file, as described in this section. Then type a new name for the file in the File Name text box (so you do not overwrite the original file by accident) and click **Save**. Windows 7 saves the file in the folder you chose, with the name you indicated.

Open a File

In addition to creating new files, you can open files that you have created and saved previously in order to continue adding data or to edit existing data.

Regardless of whether you store a file in a folder on your computer's hard drive or on a CD, you can easily access files using the Open dialog box. If you are not sure where you saved a file, you can use the Open dialog box's Search function to locate it.

When you are finished using a file, you should close it. Closing files and programs frees up processing power on your computer.

Open a File

① Click the **File** tab.

● If the file you want to open is listed under Recent Documents, you can click it to open it.

② Click **Open**.

The Open dialog box appears.

Note: *Another way to launch the Open dialog box is to press* Ctrl + O.

③ In the Navigation pane, click the library in which the file you want to open has been saved (here, **Documents**).

④ In the file list, locate and click the folder in which the file you want to open has been saved.

⑤ Click **Open**.

6 Click the name of the file that you want to open.

7 Click **Open**.

The file opens in the program window.

KO RACING

2011 Goals

How do you close a file?
To close a file, click the **File** tab and click **Exit** in the screen that appears. Alternatively, click the **Close** (☒) button in the upper-right corner of the program window. Windows 7 closes the file and the program window. Closing files frees up processing power on your computer.

What if you cannot find my file?
You can use the Search box in the upper right corner of the Open dialog box to locate files. Simply locate and open the folder in which you believe the file was saved and type the file's name in the Search box.

Print a File

If you have connected a printer to your laptop (either via a cable or through a wireless network), you can create printouts of your files. For example, you might distribute printouts of a file as handouts in a meeting.

When you print a file, you can send a file directly to the printer using the default settings, or you can open your program's Print dialog box to change these settings. For example, you might opt to print just a portion of the file, print multiple copies of a file, collate the printouts, and so on.

Print a File

1 Click the **File** tab.

● The File menu opens.

2 Position your mouse pointer over the **Print** option.

● To print the file using the default settings, click **Quick print**.

3 Click **Print**.

The Print dialog box appears.

Note: Another way to open the Print screen is to press Ctrl + P.

● You can select a printer from the **Select Printer** list.

● You can specify the number of copies to print using the **Number of Copies** spin box.

● You can select to print a selection from the file or specific pages using the available settings in the **Page Range** area.

④ Click **Print**.

The program sends the file to the printer for printing.

How do you set up a printer?
If your printer is designed to connect to your laptop via a USB cable, simply connect it to your laptop; Windows 7 detects the printer and takes the appropriate steps to set it up. If the printer uses another type of cable, connect it to the laptop, launch the Print dialog box, and double-click **Add Printer** in the Select Printer area. Windows 7 launches the Add Printer wizard; click **Add a local printer** and follow the prompts. If the printer is a network printer, follow these same steps but click **Add a network, wireless or Bluetooth printer** in the Add Printer wizard.

Install a Program

Few people limit themselves to using only the programs that came installed on their laptop. Odds are, over time you will want to install additional programs. Windows 7 is designed to make this as easy as possible.

The ins and outs of installing a program differ by program. Some programs are downloaded from the Internet (as covered in this section), others from a CD or DVD. And the precise steps required are as different as the programs themselves. Do not let this deter you from installing programs on your laptop. Windows 7 is designed to guide you step by step through the installation process.

Install a Program

① From the product's Web site, double-click the program link that you want to download.

② Click **Run** when prompted.

Windows 7 launches the InstallShield Wizard, a tool for installing programs.

③ Click **Next**.

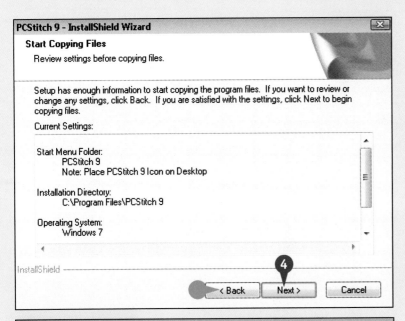

After you select the desired settings in the wizard, it gives you the opportunity to review your choices.

● To change any of your choices, click **Back**.

④ If the settings are correct as is, click **Next**.

The InstallShield Wizard informs you when setup is complete.

⑤ Click **Finish**.

Simplify It

Can you uninstall a program you no longer want?
Yes. To uninstall a program, click the **Start** button (🔵) and select **Control Panel**. In the Control Panel window, click **Uninstall a Program** under Programs. The Programs and Features window opens. Click the program you want to remove. Click **Uninstall**. Windows 7 prompts you to confirm the removal of the program.

Set Up Gadgets

Windows 7 comes bundled with several mini-programs, called *gadgets*, which you can install on the desktop.

Some gadgets broadcast information such as news headlines, weather conditions, exchange rates, and stock quotes; others offer quick access to frequently used tools such as a clock; still others, such as Windows' Slide Show

gadget (which cycles through the images in your Pictures folder) and the Picture Puzzle gadget, are designed with entertainment in mind.

Note that certain gadgets, such as those that broadcast weather or stock information, require that your laptop be connected to the Internet to work.

Set Up Gadgets

1 Right-click a blank area of the desktop.

2 Click **Gadgets**.

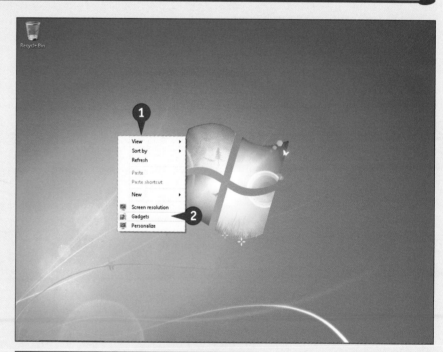

3 The Desktop Gadgets window appears. Click the gadget you want to add to your desktop.

*Note: In addition to adding the gadgets that come bundled with Windows 7, you can access additional gadgets online. To do so, click the **Get more gadgets online** link in the bottom-right corner of the Desktop Gadgets window.*

④ Drag the gadget to the spot on the desktop where you want it to appear.

⑤ Release the mouse button. The gadget is added to the desktop.

⑥ Click the Desktop Gadgets window's **Close** button (❌) to close it.

*Note: Some gadgets can be enlarged to display even more information. To enlarge your gadget, click the **Larger Size** button (▣) in the toolbar.*

Simplify It

How do you customize a gadget?
Some gadgets require a bit of customization. For example, by default, the Weather gadget displays weather information for New York, NY. If you want your gadget to display weather information for a different part of the globe, position your mouse pointer over the gadget and click the **Options** button (🔧) in the toolbar that appears. A dialog box opens; indicate your preferences for the gadget. For example, in the dialog box displayed for the Weather gadget, you indicate your current location and whether temperature should be shown in Fahrenheit or Celsius. Click **OK**. Windows updates the gadget per your specifications.

Download Programs
from Windows Live

In Windows 7, Microsoft omitted certain features that were bundled in earlier versions of the operating system. Instead, Microsoft made these features available from Windows Live (http://home.live.com).

Windows Live offers several online services, as well as access to various applications that you can download to your PC. These include

Messenger, for chatting with friends and family; Photo Gallery, for editing, organizing, and sharing photos; Mail, for reading and replying to e-mail messages; Writer, for composing blog posts; and Movie Maker, for creating videos and publishing them to the Web. You learn how to use several of these tools in later chapters.

Download Programs from Windows Live

① On the main Windows Live page, hover over Windows Live.

Note: You must be connected to the Internet and signed into the site to access this page. See the tip at the end of this section for help.

② Click **Downloads**.

The Windows Live Essentials page opens.

③ Click **Download Now**.

A File Download – Security Warning dialog box appears.

④ Click **Run**.

*Note: If prompted by the Windows 7 User Account Control dialog box to authorize the download, click **Yes**.*

Windows prompts you to specify what programs you want to install.

⑤ Ensure that the check box next to each desired program is checked.

⑥ Click **Install**.

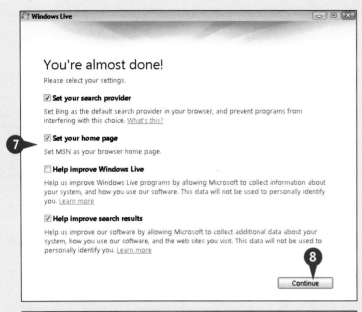

Windows installs the selected programs.

Note: *The installation may take several minutes. A progress window keeps you apprised of the status.*

When installation is complete, Windows prompts you to select your settings.

⑦ Select the appropriate check boxes to establish your settings.

⑧ Click **Continue**.

Microsoft welcomes you to Windows Live.

⑨ Click **Close**.

How do you create a Windows Live account?
Before you can download programs from Windows Live or use any of the site's features, you must set up an account and sign into the site. To set up an account, point your browser to http://home.live.com and click **Sign Up**. Next, select a Live ID, create a password, and enter an alternate e-mail address. Then enter the requested personal information, type the characters you see in the **Characters** field, and click **I Accept** to create your account. To sign into Windows Live, launch the site, type your Live ID and password, and click **Sign In**.

Chapter 4

Navigating Files and Folders in Windows 7

Windows 7 includes a program called Windows Explorer. It acts like a digital filing cabinet, with folders to store your files and programs.

Windows Explorer enables you to *manage* your files — to copy and move them, rename them as needed, and delete them when you are finished using them.

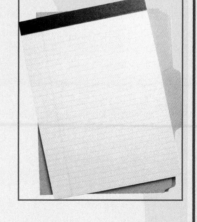

When you open a folder in Windows Explorer, it appears in its own folder window. Folder windows contain several panes to make it easier to find the files you need. They also include a toolbar with various options, as well as a Search field to help you locate the files you need.

View Files and Folders

Windows 7 includes a program called Windows Explorer. It acts like a digital filing cabinet, with folders to store and organize your files and programs. Each folder contains tools for searching, navigating, and organizing the files and subfolders within it.

Windows Explorer contains three main folders, called libraries, for storing files: the Documents library, the Pictures library, and the Music library. The Documents library is where word-processor files, spreadsheets, and Web pages are stored by default. The Pictures library acts as a central repository for digital image files. The Music library is where audio files that you download or rip are saved. In addition, Windows Explorer contains a Videos library.

View Files and Folders

1 Click **Start** (⊞).

2 Click **Documents**, **Pictures**, or **Music**.

A Windows Explorer folder window opens, displaying the contents of the library you chose.

Note: An even faster way to launch Windows Explorer is to click the Windows Explorer taskbar button (▢). The Libraries folder opens, providing quick access to the Documents, Music, and Pictures libraries, as well as to the Videos library.

Navigate Folder Windows

Folder windows in Windows Explorer contain several panes to make it easier to find the files you need. Folder windows also offer several options when it comes to how files are displayed in the Windows Explorer File list — for example, as icons of various sizes, in list form with details such as size and date created,

and so on. In addition, each folder window contains a toolbar with various buttons for organizing, sharing, and burning files; creating a new folder; changing how files in the folder window are displayed, and getting help. A Search field is also present.

Navigation Pane
This pane contains clickable links to other folders on your Windows system.

File List
Files in the selected folder are listed in the File list.

Library Pane
Here, you specify how files in the File list should be arranged — by folder, date, rating, or tag.

Preview Pane
When you click, or select, a file in the File list, a preview of that file appears in the Preview pane. (You will learn more about selecting files later in this chapter.)

Details Pane
This pane includes details about the selected file in the File list. (Specific details vary by file type.)

Folder Window Toolbar
Access folder and file options here. Note that specific options differ depending on what library is open.

Change Your View
Click the ⬛ next to the Change Your View button to select a different file view. (The appearance of this button differs depending on the currently selected file view.)

Hide the Preview Pane
Click the Hide the Preview Pane button to hide the Preview pane.

Search Box
Use the Search box to find files in the current folder. You will learn more about searching for files later in this chapter.

Open Files and Folders

One way to open a file is from within a program window, as discussed in the previous chapter. Alternatively, you can use Windows Explorer to locate and open a file.

When you open a file from within Windows Explorer, Windows 7 automatically launches the application associated with that file, and then opens the file in that application's window. For example, if the file you want to open is a Rich Text file, Windows 7 launches the WordPad application and then displays the contents of the file in the WordPad window. You can open the file in a different program if you choose, however.

Open Files and Folders

1 Double-click the folder that contains the file you want to open.

● The folder opens and its contents appear in the File list.

2 Double-click the file you want to open.

Windows opens the file in the default program.

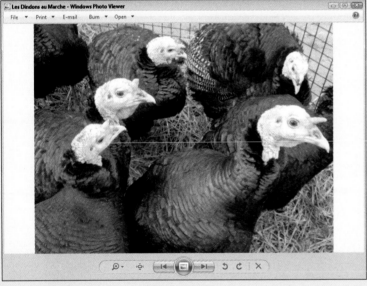

③ Alternatively, to open the file in a different program, right-click the file.

④ Click **Open with**.

⑤ Click the program you want to use to view and/or edit the file.

Windows opens the file in the program you chose.

Note: *To change the program that Windows uses to open a certain type of file by default, select* **Choose default program** *from the Open With menu, click the program you want to use in the Open With dialog box, select the* **Always use the selected program to open this kind of file** *check box, and click* **OK**.

Simplify It

How do I open files on external media?
Insert your CD or DVD and follow these steps:

① Click the **Start** button (⊞).

② Click **Computer**.

③ In the Computer directory, double-click a drive to view its contents.

④ Open the folder containing the file you want to view.

⑤ Open the file.

Create a New Folder

Windows Explorer contains several predefined folders, or libraries, such as Documents, Pictures, Music, and Videos. In addition to these, you can create your own folders. Creating folders makes it much easier to keep your files organized.

For example, you might create a subfolder in your Documents folder for one of your clients to contain any correspondence or other files that pertain to that client. Alternatively, you might create folders for each project you are working on to store all the files associated with each project, or you might create a folder to store all your photographs from a recent trip.

Create a New Folder

1 With the folder in which you want to create the new folder open in Windows Explorer, click the **New folder** button.

● Windows creates a new folder with the default name, New Folder, selected.

2 Type a descriptive name for the new folder and press Enter.

Select Files and Folders

You can use Windows Explorer to manage your files — for example, to copy them, move them, rename them, delete them, rate them, and tag them. Before you can perform any of these actions on a file, you must select the file. That way, Windows knows exactly with which file you want to work.

You can select files one at a time or select multiple files at once — useful, for example, if you want to move several files into a new folder.

Note that although the steps here cover selecting files, the technique for selecting folders is the same.

Select Files and Folders

Select a Single File

1 Click a file.

● The file is highlighted in the File list, indicating that it is selected.

● A preview of the selected file appears in the Preview pane.

Select Multiple Files

1 While pressing **Ctrl**, click each of the files you want to select.

● Each file you **Ctrl** + clicked is selected.

Note: *To select multiple files that are grouped together, click the first file in the group and, while pressing* **Shift**, *click the last item in the group. The first file, the last file, and all the files in between will be selected.*

Note: *To deselect all selected files, click an empty area in the File list. If you have selected multiple files but need to deselect only one, press and hold* **Ctrl** *and click the file you want to deselect.*

Move and Copy Files and Folders

Most likely, you will populate Windows Explorer with many files and folders over time. If you place a file in the wrong folder by accident, or simply create a new folder to store documents you have already created, you must move your files to the correct folder.

In addition to moving files, you can copy them. Copying a file creates two versions of it — one in the original location and one in the new location.

Note that the steps for moving and copying files, covered here, are the same as the steps for moving and copying folders.

Move and Copy Files and Folders

Move a File

1. Select the file(s) you want to move.

2. Click the **Organize** button.

3. Click **Cut**.

4. Open the folder into which you want to move the selected file(s).

5. Click the **Organize** button.

6. Click **Paste**.

   The selected file(s) is moved from the old location to the new one.

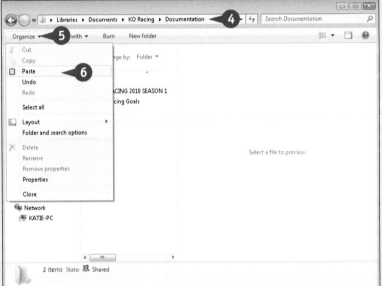

Copy a File

1 Select the file(s) you want to copy.

2 Click the **Organize** button.

3 Click **Copy**.

4 Open the folder into which you want to copy the selected file(s).

5 Click the **Organize** button.

6 Click **Paste**.

A copy of the selected file(s) is placed in the new location.

Simplify It

How do I copy a file to a CD or DVD?
If your computer has a recordable CD or DVD drive, you can copy files and folders to a recordable disc. Select the file(s) you want to copy, or burn, to disc. Click the **Burn** button in the folder window toolbar. When prompted, insert a blank disc into the drive. Windows displays the Burn a Disc dialog box; type a title for your disc. Click **Like a USB Flash Drive** to create a data CD or DVD (as opposed to a music CD or video DVD). Click **Next**. Windows formats the disc, and then copies the files.

Rename a File or Folder

Giving your files and folders descriptive names makes it easier to keep things organized. If a file or folder's current name is not adequately descriptive, you can rename it. File and folder names can be as long as 255 characters, although the following characters cannot be used:

< > , ? : \ *

You should only rename files and folders that you have created yourself or that have been given to you by others. Never rename Windows system files or folders, or files or folders associated with programs installed on your computer. Otherwise, your computer could behave erratically or even crash.

Rename a File or Folder

1 Click the file or folder you want to rename to select it.

2 Right-click the selected file or folder.

3 Click **Rename** from the menu that appears.

Windows selects the current filename or folder name.

4 Type a new name for the file or folder and press Enter.

Windows renames the file or folder.

Compress a File or Folder

Windows Explorer enables you to compress files and folders to save space. When you compress files and folders, you reduce the number of bytes they contain.

Compressing files and folders is especially useful if, for example, you need to share several files or folders with others via e-mail. Uploading and

downloading very large files is time-consuming at best, and impossible at worst. You might also compress files and folders to squeeze them onto a recordable CD or DVD.

When a compressed file or folder is uncompressed, it is identical to the original, uncompressed file or folder.

Compress a File or Folder

1 Select the file(s) or folder(s) you want to compress.

2 Right-click a selected file or folder.

3 Click **Send to**.

4 Click **Compress (zipped) folder**.

● Windows copies the selected files and/or folders, compresses the copies, and places them in a special compression folder (also called a Zip folder).

Note: *You can rename a Zip folder just like you would any other type of folder or file.*

Extract Items from a Zip Folder

Suppose you receive a Zip folder via e-mail or you have copied a Zip folder to a CD, and you need to access the files or folders it contains. To do so, you must *extract* the compressed files or folders from the Zip folder. The extracted items will be identical to the original versions, before they were compressed.

When you extract items from a Zip folder, you can specify the folder in which the extracted items should be saved. You can also instruct Windows Explorer to open the folder you choose in its own window after the extraction is complete.

Extract Items from a Zip Folder

1 Select the Zip folder containing the files you want to extract.

2 Right-click the Zip folder.

3 Click **Extract All** from the menu that appears.

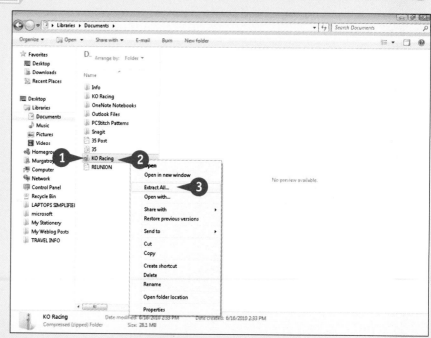

The Extract Compressed (Zipped) Folders window appears.

● You can click the **Browse** button to extract the files to a location other than the default.

4 Click **Extract**.

Windows extracts the files and/or folders into the folder you specified.

Search for Files and Folders

As you work with more and more files and folders on your PC, finding the one you need can become difficult. Fortunately, Windows Explorer offers a robust search function. If you have a general idea where the file or folder you are looking for is located — say, somewhere in your Documents folder — you can use the Search box found in the Documents folder window to search for the file or folder.

You can search using various criteria including name, file type, author, date, even words or phrases that appear within the file (assuming you are searching for a text file as opposed to a digital image or music file).

Search for Files and Folders

① Click in the **Search** box.

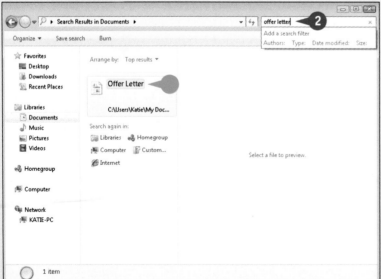

② Type part or all of the file's name, type, author, or other criteria.

● As you type, Windows displays files and folders within the current folder that match your criteria.

Sort and Filter Files

If you have lots of files in a folder, you can sort them based on various file properties. By default, files are sorted by name, but you can sort by any other property, including Date Modified, Author, Type, and so on.

You can also filter files such that only those files with a particular property value are shown in the folder window. For example, you might opt to display those files of the TIFF file type.

To sort and filter files, the folder window must be in Details view. To switch to Details view, click the Change Your View ⊡ and click Details.

Sort and Filter Files

Sort Files

1 Click the column header that contains the property by which you want to sort — for example, the Size header.

Note: *You might need to hide the Preview pane to view all available columns. To do so, click the **Hide Preview Pane** button (▣). Click the button a second time when you are again ready to reveal the pane.*

● Windows Explorer sorts the files by the property you clicked.

Note: *To switch the sort order (from ascending to descending or vice versa), simply click the column header again.*

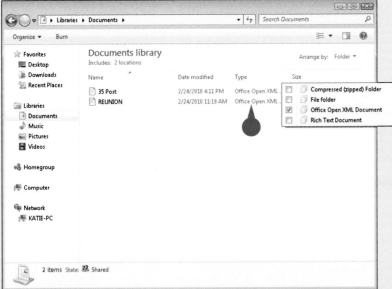

Filter Files

1 Position your mouse pointer over the column header for the property you want to filter (here, Type).

A down arrow appears on the right side of the column header.

2 Click the ⊡ to see a list of values associated with the column's property.

3 Click the check box with the property value by which you want to filter.

● Windows displays only the files with the property value you chose.

Simplify It

How do I sort by a different property?
If the column header for the property by which you want to sort or filter your files does not appear in Windows Explorer, you can add it. With the folder that contains the files you want to sort or filter open in Details view, right-click one of the existing column headings. Select the property by which you want to sort or filter from the list that appears. Alternatively, click **More** to open the Choose Details dialog box; then, click the check box next to a property to select it, and click **OK**. Windows adds a column for the property you chose.

Tag Files

Windows applies certain properties to files, such as Name, Date Modified, Author, File Type, and so on. You can use these properties as criteria when searching for files.

In addition, Windows enables you to apply tags — brief descriptions embedded in the files' metadata — to certain types of files, which you can also use as sort, filter, and search criteria. These tags could be anything you choose — the name of the person featured in a digital photo, the project with which a document is associated, and so on. The easiest way to apply a tag is to use the Windows Explorer Details pane.

Tag Files

1. Select the file you want to tag.
   - Information about the file appears in the Details pane.
2. Click **Add a tag**.
   - A blinking cursor appears in the Add a Tag field.

3. Type a tag.
4. Before adding a second tag, type a semicolon (;).

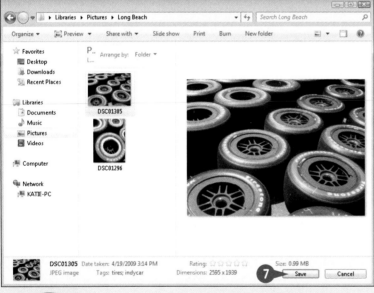

⑤ Type another tag.

● If the tag you type has already been applied to other files, a menu appears listing the tag alongside a check box.

⑥ Click the check box to select it.

⑦ Click **Save**.

Windows saves your tag(s).

Simplify It

How do you rate files?
To rate a file, follow these steps:

① Select the file you want to rate.

② In the Details pane, next to the **Rating** entry, click the star that represents the rate you want to apply. For example, to give the file a two-star rating, click the second star.

③ Click **Save**.

Delete a File or Folder

If you no longer need a file or folder, you can delete it. Deleting unwanted files and folders can help you avoid cluttering your Windows system.

As with renaming files and folders, you should delete only files and folders that you create yourself or that others have given to you; otherwise, your system may begin acting strangely or even crashing.

Deleting a file or folder moves it to the Recycle Bin, where it remains until the Recycle Bin is emptied or until Windows removes the file or folder to make room for other deleted items. As long as neither of these events has occurred, you can restore files and folders you have deleted to their original location.

Delete a File or Folder

Delete a File or Folder

① Select the file(s) or folder(s) you want to delete.

② Click the **Organize** button.

③ Click **Delete**.

Windows prompts you to confirm the deletion.

④ Click **Yes**.

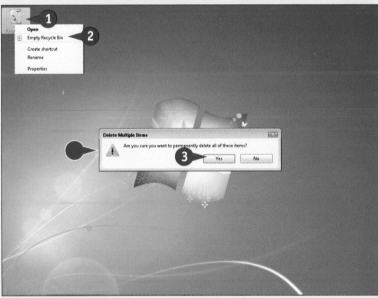

● The file is deleted from the folder window.

● The Recycle Bin icon on the desktop changes to indicate it is no longer empty.

Empty the Recycle Bin

1 Right-click the Recycle Bin icon on your desktop.

*Note: If you cannot see the desktop because you have program and/or folder windows open, click the **Show Desktop** button on the rightmost edge of the taskbar.*

2 Click **Empty Recycle Bin**.

● Windows prompts you to confirm that you want to permanently delete the files in the Recycle Bin.

3 Click **Yes**.

Windows empties the Recycling Bin.

Simplify It

How do you restore a deleted item from the Recycle Bin?
You can restore items you deleted by following these steps:

1 Right-click the Recycle Bin shortcut icon on the desktop. (If you cannot see the desktop because you have program and/or folder windows open, click the **Show Desktop** button on the rightmost edge of the taskbar.)

2 Click **Open**.

3 The Recycle Bin window appears. Select the item you want to restore.

4 Click the **Restore This Item** button in the window's toolbar.

Chapter 5

Working with Images on Your Laptop PC

Windows 7 includes several tools for working with digital images, including the Pictures folder, Windows Photo Viewer, and Paint. You can also use Windows Live Photo Gallery, a free program available from the Windows Live Web site. (Refer to Chapter 3 for help downloading Windows Live Photo Gallery.)

Although the Pictures folder, Windows Photo Viewer, and Paint have their uses, Windows Live Photo Gallery has many more features, enabling you to view, organize, and edit your digital pictures. Windows Live Photo Gallery also makes it easy to share your photos, with tools for e-mailing, printing, and posting your photos online as well as for ordering prints.

Start Windows Live Photo Gallery

After you download Windows Live Photo Gallery to your laptop PC (refer to Chapter 3 for help), you start it like you do any other program: via the Start menu.

When you start Windows Live Photo Gallery, you may be prompted to sign in to the

Windows Live Web site. Logging on to the Windows Live Web site enables you to create online photo albums that you can share with your friends and family. (You will learn how to create and share these albums later in this chapter.)

Start Windows Live Photo Gallery

① Click the **Start** button (●).

② Click **All Programs**.

③ Click **Windows Live**.

④ Click **Windows Live Photo Gallery**.

Windows launches Windows Live Photo Gallery.

● The Sign In to Windows Live dialog box appears.

● If the Sign In to Windows Live dialog box fails to appear, you can click **Sign in** to open it.

⑤ Type your Windows Live ID.

⑥ Type your Windows Live password.

⑦ Click **Sign In**.

Explore Windows Live Photo Gallery

The Windows Live Photo Gallery window looks somewhat like the Pictures folder window. It features a Navigation pane for locating the photos you want to view; a toolbar with buttons that enable you to execute various operations on your photos; a Search box to aid in finding a particular photo; and more.

That being said, the Windows Live Photo Gallery window, which displays all images stored in the Pictures folder by default, offers access to far more features and tools than the Pictures folder window. For example, in Windows Live Photo Gallery, you can edit your photos, adjusting their color and eliminating red eye as needed.

Navigation Pane

Use the Navigation pane to specify what photos should be shown. Use the Date Taken, People Tags, and Descriptive Tags categories to display only certain photos.

File List

Photos in the selected folder, taken on the specified date, or containing the people tags or descriptive tags you select, appear here.

Toolbar

The Windows Live Photo Gallery toolbar offers access to tools for fixing your photos, organizing them, publishing them, e-mailing them, and more.

Search Pane

To locate a photo with a certain tag or name or of a specific type, enter your criteria in the Search pane.

View Options

Access view options here, including options for rotating photos and zooming.

Import Images to Your Laptop PC

To view and edit your digital photos on your laptop, you must first import them from the digital camera you used to capture them.

One way to make the images stored on your camera's memory card accessible to your laptop for import is to use a cable to connect the camera directly to your computer. Another method is to remove the memory card from the camera, insert it into a memory-card reader, and then plug the memory-card reader into your PC's USB port. Alternatively, if your laptop boasts a built-in memory-card reader, simply insert the memory card into it.

Import Images to Your Laptop PC

1 Insert your memory card or connect your camera to your laptop.

2 In Windows Live Photo Gallery, click **File**.

3 Click **Import from a camera or scanner**.

The Import Photos and Videos Wizard starts.

4 Click the icon for your camera or memory card.

5 Click **Import**.

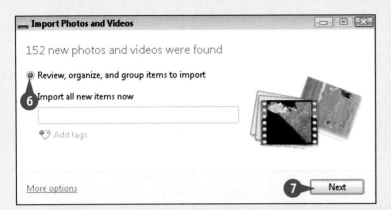

The Import Photos and Videos Wizard detects any image or video files on your camera or memory card.

⑥ Click the **Review, organize, and group items to import** option button (⦿).

⑦ Click **Next**.

⑧ Make sure the check box next to each group you want to import is checked (☑).

⑨ Click **Import**.

Windows Live Photo Gallery imports the images from your camera or memory card to your laptop.

How do you scan photos?
Many people have albums or shoeboxes stuffed with photos taken with a traditional film-based camera — holdovers from before they went digital. If you are one of these people, you can use a scanner to convert these photo prints to digital images. To do so, connect your scanner to your PC; Windows 7 should detect it and install the necessary drivers. Then place a photo print in the scanner as outlined in the scanner's manual. Finally, in Windows Live Photo Gallery, click **File**, click **Import from a camera or scanner**, click the scanner in the list of devices that appears, and click **Import**.

Batch-Rename Photo Files

In the past, people painstakingly organized their favorite photos in albums, haphazardly stashing the rest in shoeboxes. Today, digital photos can be stored, located, and viewed on your computer with the click of a button.

An important part of organizing your photos in Windows Live Photo Gallery is giving them descriptive names. This makes it easier to locate the photos you want to view and edit. To expedite this, Windows Live Photo Gallery enables you to rename image files in batches, replacing the filenames your camera creates (think "DC000591.jpg") with more meaningful names (for example, "FranceTrip2010.jpg") for several image files at once.

Batch-Rename Photo Files

1. In Windows Live Photo Gallery, select the pictures you want to batch-rename.

   Note: *To select multiple pictures, press* Ctrl *as you click each picture.*

2. Right-click a selected picture.

3. Click **Rename**.

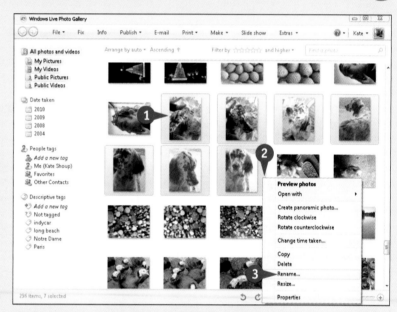

● The Info pane opens with the contents of the Filename field selected.

4. Type a name for the files and press Enter.

   Windows Live Photo Gallery applies the name to each selected picture along with a sequential number to differentiate the files.

Tag Photo Files

Just as you can apply tags to picture files in the Pictures folder window, you can apply tags using Windows Live Photo Gallery. Tags are brief descriptions embedded in the files' metadata that you can use as sort, filter, and search criteria.

In addition to applying descriptive tags in Windows Live Photo Gallery, you can apply

special people tags — that is, tags that identify the people in your photos. This makes it easier to sort and locate photos of your friends and family.

To apply a tag to a photo, you use the Windows Live Photo Gallery Info pane.

Tag Photo Files

1 In the Windows Live Photo Gallery window, select the picture or pictures you want to tag.

2 Click **Info** along the top of the window to display the Info pane.

3 Click **Add descriptive tags**.

4 Type a tag and press Enter.

Note: If adding multiple tags, separate them with a comma.

● To add a people tag, click **Add people tags**. Then select from the list of names that appears or type a new name in the blank field. To tag yourself, select **That's Me!**

View and Open Images

Windows Live Photo Gallery displays photos as thumbnail-sized images by default. You can view larger versions of your images in Windows Live Photo Gallery in a few different ways. One is to display a preview of the image; another is to open the image in its own screen. If, for example, you need to edit an image, you must open it in its own screen.

After you open an image, you can return to the main Windows Live Photo Gallery window by clicking the Back to Gallery button located in the upper-left corner of the window.

View and Open Images

1 Position your mouse pointer over the image you want to preview.

● Windows Live Photo Gallery displays a preview of the image.

2 Double-click the image.

The image opens in its own window.

Auto-Adjust a Photo

CHAPTER 5

Auto-Adjust a Photo

If an image lacks in contrast, seems slightly off colorwise, or is a bit skewed, you can use Windows Live Photo Gallery's Auto Adjust tool to fix these problems. The Auto Adjust tool automatically applies the Adjust Exposure, Adjust Color, and Straight Photo fixes at once. (Note that you can, if you prefer, apply these fixes manually on an individual basis.)

Note that before you edit an image, you should make a copy of it and preserve the original. That way, if you are unhappy with the edits, the photo is not permanently damaged.

Auto-Adjust a Photo

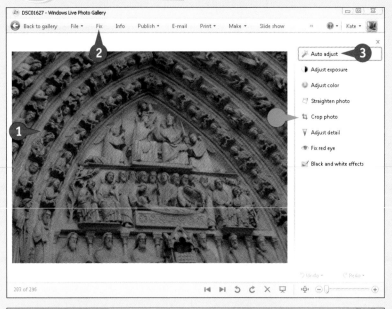

1 Open the image you want to auto-adjust.

2 Click **Fix**.

● The Fix pane opens.

3 Click **Auto adjust**.

● Windows Live Photo Gallery assesses your image, applies the necessary exposure and color settings, and straightens the image as needed.

● If clicking Auto adjust does not yield the desired results, use the Brightness, Contrast, Shadows, and Highlights sliders to adjust these settings manually.

● To access the Color Temperature, Tint, and Saturation sliders, click **Adjust color**.

99

Crop a Photo

A key aspect of image composition is ensuring that only what should appear in the image does appear in the image.

If you discover that your image contains some unwanted elements — for example, a telephone pole that appears to be growing out of your subject's head — you can crop those elements out. You might also crop an image simply to improve its composition.

When cropping an image, you can select from several preset proportions. Alternatively, you can create your own custom crop.

As always, you should make a copy of your image and preserve the original before applying your edits.

Crop a Photo

① Open the image you want to crop.

② Click **Fix**.

③ Click **Crop photo**.

● A cropping frame appears in the image.

● To change the proportion of the cropping frame, click the **Proportion** ▣ and select a preset.

● To rotate the crop frame, click **Rotate frame**.

④ Click and drag the crop frame to the desired spot on the photograph.

● To resize the crop frame, click and drag one of the sizing handles inward or outward.

⑤ Click **Apply**.

Windows Live Photo Gallery crops the photo.

Remove Red Eye

Many photos involve the use of a flash. Often, however, when you use a flash to photograph someone in ambient low light, the resulting image shows a person who appears to have red eyes. This results from the light from the flash reflecting off the fundus, which is the interior surface of the eye opposite the lens, where the retina, optic disc, macula, fovea, and posterior pole are located.

Fortunately, you can use the Fix Red Eye tool in Windows Live Photo Gallery to remove this red-eye effect and restore your demonic-looking subject to his or her angelic self.

Remove Red Eye

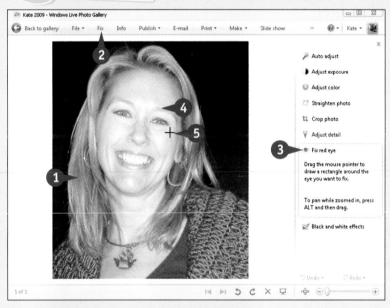

1. Open the image you want to correct.
2. Click **Fix**.
3. In the Fix pane, click **Fix red eye**.
4. Click the upper-left corner of an eye that needs correcting.
5. Drag the cursor to the lower-right corner of the eye to select the eye.

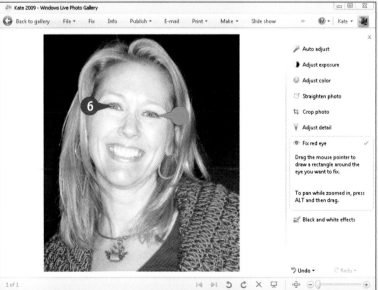

● Windows Live Photo Gallery removes the red eye.

6. Repeat Steps **4** and **5** to remove red eye from any remaining eyes in the photo.

101

Create and Publish an Online Photo Album

A great way to share your digital photos with others is to publish them in an online album on Windows Live. After you publish the album, you can e-mail a link to that album to others, who can then view and even comment on your photos. As an added benefit, publishing your photos online protects you by giving you access to copies of all your precious photos in the event your hard drive were to fail.

Note that you must be signed in to Windows Live to publish an album. If you are not signed in, click the Sign In button in the upper-right corner of the Windows Live Photo Gallery window and follow the on-screen instructions.

Create and Publish an Online Photo Album

1 In the Windows Live Photo Gallery window, select the pictures you want to include in the album.

2 Click **Publish**.

3 Click **Online album**.

The Publish Photos on Windows Live dialog box opens.

● To add the photos to an album you have already created, click it.

4 To create a new album, type a name for the album.

5 Click the album's ⊡ and select who should be permitted to view the album.

6 Click **Publish**.

Windows Live Photo Gallery uploads the selected images to the Windows Live Web site and notifies you when the upload operation is complete.

⑦ Click **View album** to view the album online.

Windows Live opens in your Web browser, with the page containing your album on display.

Note: To e-mail a link to your album to others, click **Share** and click **Send a Link**. The Send a Link screen opens; type your recipients in the To field, type a message, and click **Send**.

How do you access an online album?
Direct your Web browser to the Windows Live Web site (home.live.com), sign in to your account, click the **Photos** link, click **All Albums**, and click the album you want to view to open it.

How do you obtain prints of your digital photos?
To print a photo using your own printer, open the image you want to print in Windows Live Photo Gallery, click **Print**, and click **Print**. The Print Pictures dialog box opens; click **Print**. To order prints online, select the pictures you want to order, click **Print**, and click **Order Prints**. The Order Prints Wizard starts; click a printing provider, click **Send Pictures**, and follow the on-screen instructions.

Chapter 6

Enjoying Audio and Video on Your Laptop

Using the Windows Media Player software that comes bundled with Windows 7, you can use your laptop to organize your media collection, play back your audio and video files, listen to CDs, watch DVDs, rip music from CDs in your personal library, create playlists of your favorite songs, create mix CDs, sync your audio and video files to a portable media player, and more.

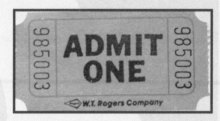

Assuming your laptop is connected to the Internet, you can also use Windows Media Player to shop for music online, listen to Internet radio broadcasts, and access video content such as movie previews.

Build Your Media Library

Audio and video files in your Windows 7 Music and Video folders appear in the Windows Media Player library by default. To further build your media library, you can use Windows Media Player to *rip*, or copy, tracks from CDs in your collection (assuming your laptop has a CD drive) or to obtain content online.

Of course, although Windows Media Player makes it easy to rip, burn, store, and organize your digital media, it is up to you to avoid copying or otherwise using copyrighted material without authorization. Unauthorized use of such materials may subject you to criminal and/or civil penalties.

Build Your Media Library

Rip Tracks from a CD

1 With Windows Media Player open, insert the CD that contains the tracks you want to rip in your computer's CD drive.

● Windows Media Player displays a list of the tracks on the CD.

● By default, all tracks on the CD are selected. To deselect a track, click its check box (☐).

2 Click **Rip CD**.

● Windows Media Player rips, or copies, the selected tracks to your music library.

Access Online Content

1 Click the ⊡ next to **Media Guide**.

2 Click **Browse all online stores**.

Windows Media Player displays a list of stores.

Note: *The stores available to you may vary depending on your location.*

3 Click a store to enter it.

Note: *Some stores offer content to which you can subscribe; with others, you purchase the content outright.*

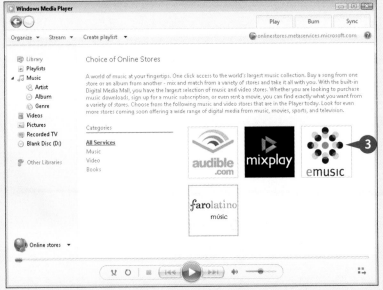

Simplify It

How do you create a store account?
Before you can purchase or subscribe to content from a Windows Media Player online store, you must first create an account with the store. The ins and outs of creating a store account differ by store. For instructions, click the Help link on a store's page.

How do you import content from a video camera?
You can import video content from a digital video camera, but not with Windows Media Player. Instead, you use Windows Live Photo Gallery. To import items, follow the steps in Chapter 5. After you import your video, it appears in Windows Media Player by default.

Find Files in Windows Media Player

Over time, your media collection may grow to the point that finding the files you want to listen to or watch may become difficult. To make it easier to find files, Windows Media Player enables you to sort them by artist, album, album artist, genre, title, release date, date taken, filename, or rating.

In addition to sorting files, you can also use Windows Media Player's Search field to search for a media file. For example, you might type the name of the song you seek; Windows Media Player then displays a list of files that match your criteria.

Find Files in Windows Media Player

Sort Files

1 Click a folder in the folder list (in this case, Music).

2 Click **Organize**.

3 Click **Sort by**.

4 Select the parameter by which you want to sort.

● Windows Media Player sorts the files in the File list.

Note: *An even faster way to sort music files is to click the □ to the left of the Music folder in the folder list; then click* **Artist**, **Album***, or* **Genre***. Windows Media Player sorts your files in the File list accordingly.*

Search for a File

1 Type a keyword or phrase in the Search field.

● Windows Media Player displays a list of files that match your criteria in the File list.

How do you rate media files?
You can apply a rating to a file in Windows Media Player. You can then sort files by rating. The program uses a five-star rating system, with five stars being the highest rating. To rate a file in Windows Media Player, simply locate it in the File list and click the star in the Rating column that represents the rating you want to apply. For example, to give the file a two-star rating, click the second star. If no rating column is shown, right-click the file you want to rate, click **Rate** in the menu that appears, and then click the appropriate star.

Listen to Music on Your Laptop

You can use Windows Media Player to listen to music on your laptop in a few different ways. One approach is to play back audio files stored on your laptop's hard drive. Assuming you have located the song or album you want to hear in Windows Media Player, playing it is as simple as clicking a button. Alternatively, if your laptop has a CD drive, you can insert a CD into the CD drive and use Windows Media Player to listen to tracks on that CD. You use the same controls when playing a music CD as you do when playing back music files on your hard drive. You can also use Windows Media Player's Media Guide feature to access Internet radio stations.

Listen to Music on Your Laptop

Listen to Music on Your Hard Drive

1. Click the **Music** folder.

2. Double-click the song or album you want to hear.

Windows Media Player plays back the song or album.

● The **Play** button (▶) changes to a **Pause** button (⏸).

● Drag the **Volume** slider to adjust the volume.

● To mute the volume, click the **Mute** button (🔊). The Mute button changes to a **Sound** button (🔊); click it to unmute the volume.

> **Note:** To listen to music while performing other tasks on your laptop, click the **Switch to Now Playing** button (▦). To switch back, click the **Switch to Library** button (▦).

- To shuffle the order in which songs are played back, click the **Shuffle** button (⊠).

- To play back a song or play list more than once, click the **Repeat** button (⟳).

- To stop playback, click the **Stop** button (▣).

- To return to the previous song, click the **Back** button (◄◄).

- To skip to the next song, click the **Next** button (►►).

Play a CD

1. With Windows Media Player open, insert into your computer's CD drive the CD that contains the tracks you want to hear.

- Windows Media Player displays a list of the tracks on the CD.

  By default, all tracks on the CD are selected. To deselect a track, click its check box (☐).

  Windows Media Player automatically plays back the selected songs on the CD.

How do you access Internet radio?

1. Click the **Media Guide** button in the bottom left of the Windows Media Player window. (If this button is not visible, click the ⊡ next to the **Online Stores** button and select **Media Guide** from the menu that appears.)

2. Click the **Internet Radio** link.

3. Click a genre. (If the genre you seek is not shown, click the **Show All Genres** link.)

4. In the Media Guide, click a station's **Listen** link to listen.

Watch Video Content on Your Laptop

As with audio, you can watch videos in a few different ways in Windows Media Player: by playing back the video files stored on your computer's hard drive or by playing a DVD you have inserted into your computer's DVD drive. You can also use Windows Media Player's Media Guide feature to access video content online.

When you play a video, Windows Media Player automatically switches to Now Playing mode; to view the player controls, simply position your mouse pointer over the Now Playing window. As you probably guessed, you use the same controls to play back videos as you do to play back music.

Watch Video Content on Your Laptop

Watch Videos on Your Hard Drive

1 Click the **Videos** folder.

2 Double-click the video you want to watch.

Windows Media Player plays back the video in Now Playing mode.

Note: You use the same controls when playing a video file as you do when playing back music files.

Play a DVD

1. With Windows Media Player open, insert into your computer's DVD drive the DVD you want to watch.

2. If the DVD menu does not appear automatically, right-click the DVD in the folder list.

3. Click **Play**.

Windows Media Player displays the DVD menu in Now Playing mode.

4. Select the desired option from the DVD menu.

● To view the DVD in full-screen mode, click the **View Full Screen** button (▣).

How do you access online video content?

1. Click the **Media Guide** button in the bottom left of the Windows Media Player window, or click the ▾ next to the **Online Stores** button and select **Media Guide** from the menu that appears.

2. Click a link on the main page to view its associated content.

3. Select an option from the menu.

4. Click a link in the page that appears to view its associated content.

Create and Save Playlists

If you want to listen to more than just a single song or a single album or watch multiple videos in a row, you can stack up files in a playlist. Windows Media Player then plays the songs or videos in your playlist in the order you specify.

If you develop a playlist you particularly like, you can save it. When you save a playlist, you can then open it in a later session to listen to the set of songs or view the videos it contains. You can also burn saved playlists to CD or DVD.

Create and Save Playlists

① Click the **Play** tab to display it.

● If the Play tab already contains other items, click **Clear list** to remove them.

② Click an audio or video file you want to include in your playlist.

③ Drag the selected file to the Play tab.

● Windows Media Player adds the item to the playlist and begins playing it back.

④ Add more files to the playlist.

● To sort the playlist, click the **List Options** button (☑), click **Sort List By**, and select a sort parameter (for example, Title).

Note: To move a file in the playlist, click it and drag it to the desired location in the list.

*Note: To remove a file from the playlist, right-click it and select **Remove from List** from the menu that appears.*

⑤ Click **Save list**.

⑥ Type a name for the playlist and press Enter.

How do you play back a playlist?
To play a saved playlist, click the **Playlists** entry in the folder pane, click the playlist you want to play, and click the **Play** button. When you play back files in a playlist, you use the same controls as when you play back a video, song, or album.

How do you delete a playlist?
To delete a playlist, click the **Playlists** entry in the folder pane, right-click the playlist you want to delete, and select **Delete** from the menu that appears. Specify whether the playlist should be deleted from your library only or from your library and your computer; then click **OK**.

Burn CDs and DVDs

If your laptop has a CD/DVD drive capable of recording to disc, you can use Windows Media Player to create an audio CD that can be played back on any standard CD player.

In addition, you can burn music as data files to a disc; this enables you to fit many more songs on a single disc. You can also burn video files in this way. When you burn audio or video files to disc as data files, they can be played back only on a computer or other device that supports the data format used.

Burn CDs and DVDs

① Click the **Playlists** folder.

② Right-click the playlist you want to burn to a disc.

③ Click **Add to**.

④ Select **Burn list**.

Note: Another way to specify what files to burn is to click the **Burn** tab to open it and then simply drag items from your Windows Media Player library into it.

Windows Media Player opens the Burn tab, with the contents of the playlist shown.

⑤ Click **Start burn**.

Windows Media Player prompts you to insert a blank disc.

6 Insert a blank recordable disc into your laptop's CD/DVD drive.

Windows Media Player burns the contents of the Burn tab onto the blank disc. (Note that this may take several minutes.)

● Windows Media Player tracks the progress of the burn operation.

Note: *If the contents of the Burn tab will not fit on a single disc, Windows Media Player gives you the option of burning the remaining items on a second blank disc.*

Can you use Windows Media Player to burn DVDs for playback on a standard DVD player?
No. You cannot use Windows Media Player to create DVDs for playback on a standard DVD player. You can, however, use Windows DVD Maker, also included with Windows 7. See that program's help information for details.

How do you burn data files to a CD or DVD?
To burn song or video files to disc as data files, repeat Steps **1** to **4** in this section. Then click the **Burn options** button in the Burn tab and select **Data CD or DVD** from the menu that appears. Next, click **Start burn** and insert a blank disc when prompted; Windows Media Player burns the files to disc.

Sync a Mobile Device with Windows Media Player

Some portable media players and mobile phones can be synced with Windows Media Player. To find out whether your device is compatible, simply connect it to your laptop using the cable provided while Windows Media Player is running.

If the device is compatible, has a storage capacity of more than 4GB, and has room to store your entire Windows Media Player library, it syncs automatically (although you can opt to sync only certain playlists if you prefer). All you need to do is click the Finish button that appears when the automatic sync is complete. Otherwise, you must sync manually, as covered here.

Sync a Mobile Device with Windows Media Player

1. Right-click the playlist, song, album, video, or other media file that you want to sync to a mobile device.

2. Click **Add to**.

3. Select **Sync list**.

Note: Another way to specify what files to sync is to click the **Sync** tab to open it and then simply drag items from your Windows Media Player library into it.

- Windows Media Player opens the Sync tab, with the item you specified shown.

Note: You can add more files to the Sync tab as needed.

4. Connect your mobile device to your laptop using the cable provided.

5. If necessary, turn the device on.

6. Click **Start sync**.

Windows Media Player syncs the contents of the Sync tab to the mobile device. (Note that this may take several minutes.)

● Windows Media Player tracks the progress of the sync operation.

● Windows Media Player notifies you when the sync is complete.

● Click **Click here** to view what files were synced.

Simplify It

How do you omit a playlist from an automatic sync?
With your mobile device powered on and connected to your laptop, click the **Sync** tab, click the **Sync options** button, and select **Set Up Sync** from the menu that appears. Then, in the Windows Media Player Device Setup dialog box, click the playlist you want to omit in the Playlists to Sync list, click **Remove**, and click **Finish**.

What portable devices are supported?
Windows Media Player cannot sync with the Microsoft Zune player. Nor can it sync with Apple's iPod or iPhone. However, several Sony devices are compatible, as are devices by Samsung and SanDisk and various types of Windows Mobile devices.

Chapter 7

Word Processing in Windows 7

Windows 7 includes a simple word-processing tool called WordPad. WordPad functions like a light version of a commercial word-processing program.

You can use WordPad to handle all your basic word-processing needs, such as viewing documents, writing letters, addressing envelopes, keeping a journal, making lists, and so on. You can dress up your WordPad documents by applying different fonts and colors and adjusting spacing, indents, and other page properties.

WordPad works with several types of document file formats. WordPad saves files in RTF (Rich Text Format) by default.

Enter and Edit Text in WordPad

When you launch WordPad or create a new WordPad file, a blank document appears in the WordPad window. (For help creating new files, see Chapter 3.) In the top left corner of that blank document is a blinking cursor, or insertion point, waiting for you to start typing.

Of course, the beauty of any word-processing program is that it enables you to easily edit your text after you type it, and WordPad is no exception. With WordPad, you can add new text or delete existing text with the greatest of ease.

Enter and Edit Text in WordPad

Type Text

1 Start typing your text.

● WordPad automatically wraps the text to the next line for you.

● The cursor marks the current location where text will appear when you start typing again.

2 Press **Enter** to start a new paragraph.

● You can press **Enter** twice to add an extra space between paragraphs.

● You can press **Tab** to quickly create an indent for a line of text.

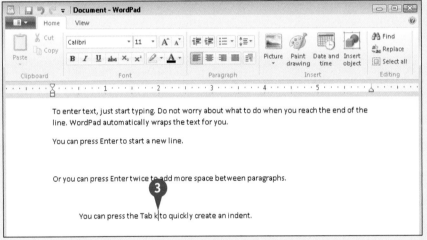

Edit Text

1 Click in the document where you want to fix a mistake and start typing.

2 Press `Backspace` to delete characters to the left of the cursor.

3 Press `Delete` to delete characters to the right of the cursor.

You can also delete selected text.

Are there special tools for blogging?
A blog is a type of Web site that enables an individual or group to share feelings, insights, and opinions — without having to learn how to use HTML or a Web editor such as FrontPage. You can create and maintain your own blog — for example, to keep in touch with friends and family or to further your career — using Windows Live Writer, an easy-to-use blogging tool from Microsoft that acts like a word processor. You can download Windows Live Writer free of charge from Microsoft's Windows Live Web site. (For help downloading Windows Live Writer, refer to Chapter 3.)

Select
Text

Before you can perform different operations on text — such as deleting it, changing its font or alignment, formatting it as a list, copying and pasting it elsewhere in a document or in a different document altogether, and so on — you must select the text. Selected text appears highlighted.

You can select text in a few different ways, using your mouse or your keyboard to select a single character, a word, a sentence, a paragraph, or all the text in the document. In this section, you learn how to drag your mouse to select text.

Select Text

① Click to one side of the word or character that you want to select.

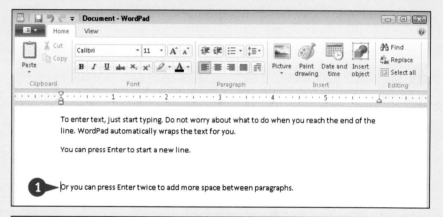

② Click and drag the cursor across the text that you want to select.

WordPad selects any characters that you drag across.

● To deselect selected text, simply click anywhere outside the text.

Move and Copy Text

Move and Copy Text (Chapter 7)

You can use the Cut, Copy, and Paste commands to move or copy text in WordPad. For example, you might cut or copy a paragraph from a WordPad document and paste it elsewhere in the same WordPad document or in another WordPad document.

When you cut text, it is removed from its original location; when you copy text, WordPad makes a duplicate of the selected data, leaving it in its original location.

Move and Copy Text

1. Select the text you want to move or copy.

2. To move the text, click **Cut**. WordPad removes the selected text from the document.

● To copy, rather than cut, the text, click **Copy**. WordPad copies the selected text, leaving it in its original location.

3. Click the spot in the document (or other WordPad window) where you want to paste the cut or copied text.

4. Click **Paste**.

● The text you cut or copied is pasted in at the specified location.

125

Change the Appearance of Text

You can change the text font, size, and color to alter the appearance of text in a document. For example, if you are creating an invitation, you might make the description of the event a different font and color to stand out from the other details. Likewise, if you are creating a report for work, you might make the title of the report larger than the information contained in the report, or even color-code certain data in the report.

In addition, you can use WordPad's basic formatting commands — Bold, Italic, Underline, Strikethrough, Subscript, and Superscript — to quickly add formatting to your text.

Change the Appearance of Text

Change the Font

1. Select the text you want to format.

2. Click the **Home** tab.

3. Click the **Font** ▼.

4. Click a font.

● WordPad applies the font to the text.

Change the Size

1. Select the text you want to format.

2. Click the **Home** tab on the Ribbon.

3. Click the **Font Size** ▼.

4. Click a size.

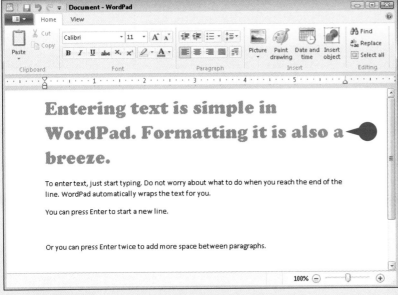

● WordPad applies the font size to the text.

*Note: Another way to change the font size is to click the **Grow Font** button (A) or the **Shrink Font** button (A) on the Home tab.*

Change the Color

① Select the text you want to format.

② Click the **Home** tab on the Ribbon.

③ Click the ⏷ next to the **Font Color** button (A).

④ Click a color.

● WordPad applies the color to the text.

How do you apply formatting to your text?
To apply formatting to your text, select the text you want to format, click the **Home** tab, and then click the **Bold** (B), **Italic** (I), **Underline** (U), **Strikethrough** (abc), **Subscript** (X₂), or **Superscript** (x²) button. WordPad applies the format you chose to the selected text.

How do you apply list formatting?
To format text as a numbered or bulleted list, select the text you want to change, then click the ⏷ next to the **Start a List** button (☰) and select a bulleted or numbered list option from the list that appears. WordPad formats the selected text as a list.

Position Text

You can use WordPad's alignment commands to change how text is positioned horizontally on a page, left-aligning text (the default), centering it, right-aligning it, or justifying it.

Indents are another way of controlling the positioning of text in a document. For example, you might indent a paragraph such as a long quote to set it apart from the rest of the text on the page.

Finally, you can adjust the amount of spacing that appears between lines of text in your paragraphs. For example, you might set double-spacing to allow for handwritten edits in your printed document.

Position Text

Align Text

1. Select the text you want to align.
2. Click the **Home** tab.
3. Click an alignment button.

● Click **Align Left** (▤) to left-align text.

● Click **Center** (▤) to center text.

● Click **Align Right** (▤) to right-align text.

● Click **Justify** (▤) to justify text between the left and right margins.

● WordPad aligns the text.

Indent Text

1. Select the paragraph(s) you want to indent.
2. Click the **Home** tab.
3. Click an indent button.

● Click **Decrease Indent** (▤) to decrease the indentation.

● Click **Increase Indent** (▤) to increase the indentation.

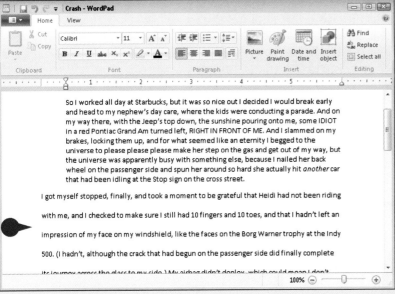

● WordPad indents the text.

Set Line Spacing

1 Select the paragraph(s) whose spacing you want to change.

2 Click the **Home** tab.

3 Click the **Line Spacing** button (▤).

4 Click a line-spacing option.

● WordPad applies the new spacing.

Simplify It

Can you set a custom indent?
You can set a custom indent using the WordPad ruler. To do so, simply drag the indent marker (▣) on the ruler to the desired location. If the ruler is not shown in the WordPad window, click the **View** tab and select the **Ruler** check box (☑).

How do you undo your changes?
If you realize you have made a change to your document in error, you can undo it. Simply click the **Undo** button (▣) in the Windows 7 Quick Access toolbar. If, after undoing a change, you realize you want to redo it, click the **Redo** button (▣) on the Quick Access toolbar.

Find and Replace Text

Suppose you are writing a story and you decide to change the main character's name. Or perhaps you realize after writing a report for work that you have consistently misspelled the name of the product you analyzed. Either way, you can use WordPad's Replace tool to rectify the situation.

If you simply need to find text rather than replace it, you can use the Find tool. For example, if you need to review a section of your document that is several pages down, you can use the Find tool to search for the title of that section instead of scrolling down to locate the section.

Find and Replace Text

1 Click the **Home** tab.

2 Click **Replace**.

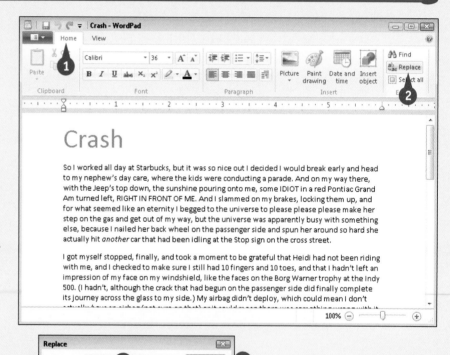

The Replace dialog box opens.

3 In the **Find what** field, type the word or phrase you want to find.

4 In the **Replace with** field, type the replacement text.

● Select the **Match whole word only** check box (☑) to find instances of the whole word only.

● Select the **Match case** check box (☑) to find instances of the word with the same capitalization.

5 Click **Find Next**.

● WordPad locates and highlights the first instance of the word or phrase you typed in the Find What field.

6 Click **Replace** to replace only the highlighted text with the word or phrase in the Replace With field.

● Click **Replace All** to replace all instances of the highlighted text with the Replace With text.

● WordPad replaces the selected text with the Replace With text.

● WordPad highlights the next instance of the text in the Find What field.

7 Repeat Step **6** until all instances of the text in the Find What field have been reviewed and/or replaced.

Note: *WordPad notifies you when it has finished searching the document for the text in the Find What field; click **OK**.*

How do I find text without replacing it?
If you simply need to find text rather than replace it, click the **Find** button in the Ribbon. The Find dialog box opens; type the word or phrase you want to find in the **Find what** field. Change the **Match whole word only** and **Match case** settings if needed; then click **Find Next**. WordPad locates and highlights the first instance of the word or phrase you typed in the Find What field. If necessary, continue clicking **Find Next** until you locate the passage you need. When you are finished searching for text, click the Find dialog box's **Close** button ([×]) to close it.

Chapter 8

Exploring the Internet and the World Wide Web with Your Laptop

The Internet and the World Wide Web have revolutionized how we communicate, conduct business, socialize, get information, and learn.

Although many people use the terms *Internet* and *World Wide Web* interchangeably, they are two different things. *Internet* refers to a global system of interconnected computer networks; *World Wide Web* describes the massive storehouse of information that resides on that system of interconnected networks. This information is presented on Web sites, which are collections of Web pages that relate to a particular person, business, government, school, or organization. You access Web pages using a special computer program called a Web browser.

Explore the Internet and the World Wide Web

The Internet is a massive network of interconnected computers that spans the globe. The enormous amount of information that resides on this network of interconnected computers is the World Wide Web.

This linked collection of data, composed of text, images, and other files, is stored on special computers called Web servers and is presented in the form of Web sites. Web sites are composed of Web pages, which users can access using a special program called a Web browser. Each Web page on the World Wide Web has its own distinct address, also called a uniform resource locator, or URL.

Web Page

Information on the Web is organized into Web pages. A Web page may include text, images, sounds, and even videos. There are literally billions of Web pages on the World Wide Web, centered on almost every imaginable topic. These Web pages are created by individuals, businesses, governments, and other organizations.

Web Site

A collection of Web pages offered by an individual, business, government, or other organization is called a Web site. There are many types of Web sites: community Web sites, corporate Web sites, e-commerce Web sites, forums, news Web sites, personal Web sites, social-networking Web sites, Web portals, wiki Web sites, and more. You might visit a Web site for a variety of reasons, such as to find information about a particular topic, to socialize, to buy or sell products, to play online games, or to attend a distance-learning class. Together, all publicly available Web sites comprise the World Wide Web. Note that some Web sites require users to pay for a subscription to access their content.

Web Server

Web sites are stored on Web servers. A Web server is simply a computer running special software. Web servers serve Web pages to Web browsers, enabling users to browse their contents. More powerful Web servers can be set up to handle heavy traffic, such as thousands of visitors, at any point in time.

Web Browser

A Web browser is a type of software program that you use to find, display, and interact with Web pages on the World Wide Web. Examples of Web browsers include Apple Safari, Google Chrome, Mozilla Firefox, Opera, and Internet Explorer. (Because Internet Explorer is included with Windows 7, it will be the Web browser discussed in this chapter.)

Web Address

Each Web page on the World Wide Web has its own unique Web address, also called a uniform resource locator, or URL. Your Web browser uses a Web page's Web address to locate the page. You can type a Web address into the Address bar of your Web browser to display the corresponding Web page. Many Web addresses are fairly intuitive; for example, many company Web sites include the company's name.

http://www.theflyingcupcakebakery.com/

URLs in Detail

A URL usually consists of four parts. The first is the scheme name, or protocol, such as http for Hypertext Transfer Protocol or ftp for File Transfer Protocol. The second part of the URL is the host name of the computer where the page is located, called the third-level domain. An example is www, for World Wide Web. The third part of the URL is the domain name, such as Amazon or IRS. The fourth part of the URL is the Web site top-level domain, such as .com for a business, .edu for a school, or .gov for a government site. For example, a typical URL would be http://www.theflyingcupcakebakery.com.

Internet Service Providers

To connect to the Internet, you must establish an account with an Internet service provider (ISP), sometimes called an Internet access provider. Examples of Internet service providers include AT&T, Comcast, and Verizon. In addition to offering customers a connection to the Internet, many Internet service providers also provide customers with e-mail accounts as well as other services, such as space on servers to back up data files. Although you can connect to the Internet using a phone line (called a dial-up connection), these types of connections are very slow and practically obsolete; higher-speed technologies such as DSL and cable are strongly recommended. You can also connect to the Internet through a wireless network, or hot spot, often found in airports and hotels.

Connect to the Internet

Before you can use your laptop to access the World Wide Web, you must connect it to the Internet. To do so, you must establish an account with an Internet service provider (ISP) such as AT&T, Comcast, or Verizon.

Usually, when you obtain an account with a broadband Internet service provider, a

technician is sent to your home to set up the Internet connection. If not, you can set up the connection yourself using the Windows 7 Connect to the Internet Wizard. This section shows you how to launch the Connect to the Internet Wizard.

Connect to the Internet

1 Connect the modem (provided by the ISP) to your computer.

Note: Make sure the modem is also plugged in to a power supply and to the appropriate jack in your wall.

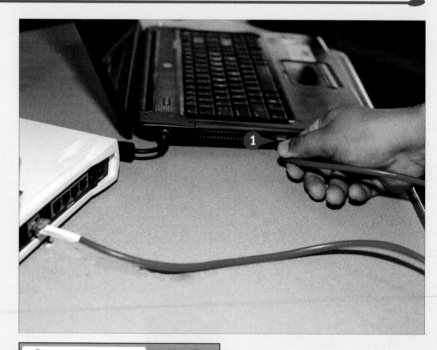

2 Click the **Start** button (⊞).

3 Click **Control Panel**.

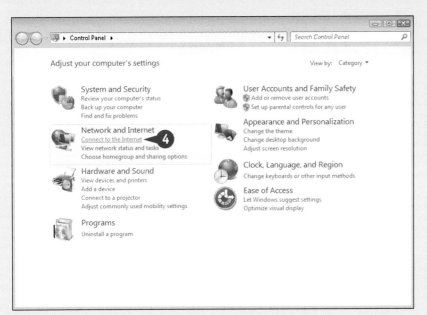

The Control Panel window opens.

④ In the Network and Internet section, click **Connect to the Internet**.

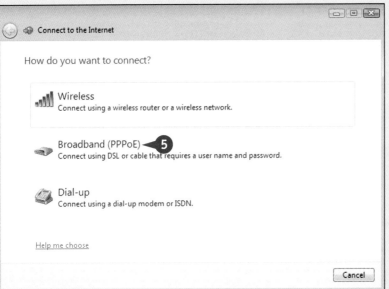

Windows launches the Connect to the Internet Wizard.

⑤ Follow the on-screen prompts (obtain the username and password from your ISP).

Simplify It

Why are connection speeds important?
With a fast Internet connection, data can be sent over the Internet and Web pages can be displayed more quickly. Where dial-up connection speeds tend to max out at 56 kilobits per second (Kbps), most broadband connections average around 500 to 600 Kbps.

How do you connect via WiFi?
If your laptop has a wireless card, you may be able to connect to the Internet via a wireless network, or a WiFi connection. Wireless networks are often found in public places such as hotels, libraries, and cafes, as well as in homes and businesses. Chapter 11 covers setting up and connecting to a wireless network.

Navigate the Internet Explorer 8 Browser

A Web browser is a software application that you use to locate and view Web pages. There are several Web browsers, each providing their own set of features. (Be aware that some Web browsers may display Web page features differently.) Examples of Web browsers include Apple's Safari, Mozilla Firefox, Opera, and Microsoft Internet Explorer.

Laptop PCs running Windows 7 come with the latest version of Internet Explorer preinstalled. (As of this writing, the latest version of Internet Explorer is Internet Explorer 8.) You start Internet Explorer 8 by clicking the program's icon in the Start menu or the taskbar.

Navigation Buttons

Click the **Back** (◙) button to return to the last page you viewed. Click the **Forward** (◙) button to redisplay the page shown when you clicked the **Back** button.

Address Bar

Type the Web address of the page you want to visit in the Address bar.

Refresh and Stop Buttons

Click the **Refresh** button (⟳) to ensure that the page you see contains the most up-to-date information. Click the **Stop** button (⊠) to stop the page-loading process.

Search Box

Type a keyword or phrase in the Search box and press `Enter` to find related Web sites and pages.

Favorites

Click the **Favorites** button to open the Favorites Center, where you can view a list of favorite sites.

Quick Tabs

Quick Tabs enable you to open multiple Web pages within a single browser window. Each page is displayed in a tab.

Links

Links often appear as colored, underlined text. You can click a link to open a new Web page. Buttons and images can also function as links.

Toolbar

The Windows Explorer 8 toolbar includes buttons for changing the home page (the page displayed by default), e-mailing pages, printing pages, accessing page options, and more.

Open a Web Page

You can open a Web page in Internet Explorer 8 using a variety of techniques. For example, you can click a link on a Web page to open a new page. Or, if you have recently visited the Web page, you may be able to access it by right-clicking the Internet Explorer button on the taskbar and choosing the page from the list that appears. Otherwise, if you know the page's Web address, you can simply enter it in the Address bar. If you do not know the page's Web address, you can search for the page; see the section "Search the Web" for help.

Open a Web Page

① In the Address bar, type the URL of the Web page you want to visit.

● As you type a Web page's address in the Address bar, Internet Explorer displays a list of URLs.

② If the URL for the page you want to visit appears, you can click it in the list.

③ If the URL does not appear, type it in its entirety and press Enter.

● Internet Explorer 8 displays the Web page whose address you entered.

Browse with Quick Tabs

Suppose you want to use the Internet to compare the price of lodging on various hotel Web sites. In earlier versions of Internet Explorer, you had to open a separate browser window for each site and switch among them, which was often a hassle.

To address this, Microsoft developed a feature called Quick Tabs. With Quick Tabs, you can open multiple Web pages at once within a single browser window, displaying each in its own tab. To switch to a different page, simply click its tab. When you are finished with a page, you can close its tab.

Browse with Quick Tabs

Launch a Page in a New Tab

1 Click the blank tab that appears to the right of any populated tabs.

● A blank tab opens.

2 Type the URL for the page you want to open in the new tab.

● The page opens.

Open a Link in a Tab

① Right-click the link whose page you want to view in its own tab.

② Click **Open Link in New Tab**.

Note: An even faster way to open a link in a new tab is to click the link while pressing and holding Ctrl.

● A tab for the new page appears.

Note: This new tab is the same color as the tab containing the link, making it easy to see which open tabs are part of the same group.

③ Click the tab to view the page.

● To close a tab, click its **Close** button (⊠).

Simplify It

Are there other ways to switch tabs?
Yes. Click the **Quick Tabs** button (⊞) to the left of the tabs to view previews of all the pages currently open in your browser window; then click a preview to switch to the corresponding tab. Alternatively, click the ▾ to the right of the **Quick Tabs** button (⊞) to view a list of all available tabs; then click a tab in the list to open it. A third option is to position your mouse pointer over the **Internet Explorer** button (⊞) on the taskbar. Previews of each open tab appear. Click the desired tab's preview to display it in your browser window.

Search the Web

You will often want to perform searches to locate Web pages of interest. You could direct your Web browser to a search engine Web site, such as www.bing.com or www.google.com, but an easier approach is to use the Internet Explorer 8 Search box.

When searching, using more specific keywords or phrases yields more targeted results. For

example, instead of simply using the keyword *motorcycle*, try *Ducati Monster 1100 S*. To search for a specific phrase, surround it with quotation marks.

You can also use Internet Explorer 8 to search for a specific word or phrase within an open Web page in your browser window.

Search the Web

Search for a Web Page

1 Type a keyword or phrase in the Internet Explorer 8 window's Search box.

● As you type, Internet Explorer displays a list of suggestions of topics that match your text.

2 If the topic you are searching for appears in the list, click it.

3 If the topic you want does not appear, type your text in its entirety and press Enter.

Internet Explorer launches Bing, with the results of your search shown in list form.

4 Click a link in the search results list.

Windows displays the page whose link you clicked.

Search for Text in a Web Page

① Type a keyword or phrase in the Internet Explorer 8 window's Search box.

② Click the down arrow to the right of the **Search** box.

③ Click **Find on this Page**.

● The Find bar appears, with the text you typed displayed.

● Internet Explorer highlights matching text on the page in yellow.

④ Click **Next** to locate the next match; click **Previous** to find the previous instance.

● Click the **Options** ⊡ and click **Match Whole Word Only** or **Match Case** to narrow your search accordingly.

Simplify It

Can you use other search tools?
Yes. In addition to using other Web search engines such as Google, you can use search tools that provide results relating to shopping, sports, movies, news, and more. To make a tool available for use, click the **Search** ⊡, click **Find More Providers**, and click a tool's **Add to Internet Explorer** button in the list that appears. In the Add Search Provider dialog box, optionally click the **Make this my default search provider** check box (☑), then click **Add**. To search using the alternative provider, type a keyword or phrase in the **Search** box, click the **Search** ⊡, and then click the provider from the menu that appears.

Keep Track of Your Favorite Pages

Boasting literally billions of Web pages, the Internet is without question an incredible resource for information. Its sheer scope, however, can make finding the information you need a chore.

When you do find a page that you know you will want to revisit, you can use Internet

Explorer 8 to mark that page as a favorite. When you mark a page as a favorite, Internet Explorer 8 saves it in a special list, called the Favorites list. When you are ready to revisit the page, you can simply click the page's entry in the list.

Keep Track of Your Favorite Pages

Save a Page as a Favorite

1 Open the page you want to save as a favorite.

2 Click the **Favorites** button.

● The Favorites Center opens.

3 Click **Add to Favorites**.

The Add a Favorite dialog box opens.

4 Type a name for the favorite.

5 Click ⊡ and select the folder in which you want to save the favorite.

6 Alternatively, to save the favorite in a new folder, click **New Folder**.

7 In the Create a Folder dialog box, type a name for the new folder.

8 Click ⊡ and select the folder in which you want to save this new folder.

9 Click **Create**.

10 Click **Add**.

The page is added to your favorites.

Open a Favorite

① Click the **Favorites** button.

② If necessary, click the **Favorites** tab.

③ If the page you want to visit has been saved in a folder, click the folder.

④ Click the page you want to visit.

● The page opens and the Favorites Center closes.

Note: To keep the Favorites Center open, click the **Pin the Favorites Center** button (⊞) before you click the site you want to visit.

Note: To delete a favorite, right-click it in the favorites list and click **Delete** in the menu that appears. Internet Explorer 8 prompts you to confirm the deletion; click **Yes**.

Simplify It

How do you save a favorite to the Favorites bar?
If the page you want to save as a favorite is one you access on a daily basis, you might prefer to save it on your Favorites bar, located immediately below the Address bar. To add a favorite to the Favorites bar, you simply open the desired page and click the **Add to Favorites Bar** button (⊞). A button for the page appears under the Internet Explorer 8 Address bar. You delete pages from the Favorites bar the same way you delete them from the Favorites Center. (Click the Favorites Bar folder to locate the desired page.)

Change Your Home Page

If you frequently visit a particular Web page, such as a news site, you can direct Internet Explorer 8 to open that page by default anytime you launch the program or click the browser's Home button. This saves you the trouble of typing the site's URL in the Address bar or selecting the site from your Favorites list.

If you want, you can set multiple home pages — for example, a national news site, a local news site, a stock ticker — to launch automatically at start up or when you click the Home button.

Change Your Home Page

Add a Single Home Page

1 With the page you want to set as your home page open in the Internet Explorer 8 window, click the ⊡ to the right of the **Home** button (🏠).

2 Click **Add or Change Home Page**.

The Add or Change Home Page dialog box appears.

3 Click the **Use this webpage as your only home page** option button (◉).

4 Click **Yes**.

Windows sets the current page as your home page.

Add Multiple Home Pages

1. With the pages you want to set as your home pages open in the Internet Explorer 8 window, click the ⬇ to the right of the **Home** button (🏠).

2. Click **Add or Change Home Page**.

The Add or Change Home Page dialog box appears.

3. Click the **Use the current tab set as your home page** option button.

4. Click **Yes**.

Windows sets the current tab set as your home page.

Note: If you no longer want to launch a page at start up, click the ⬇ to the right of the Home button (🏠) and click Remove. Then click the page you no longer want to launch at start up.

Simplify It

What is the History list?
The History list keeps track of sites you have visited. One way to view your History list is to click the ⬇ on the right side of the Address bar; Internet Explorer 8 displays a list of recently visited Web pages. You can click a page in the list to open it. To view even more pages in your History list, click the **Favorites** button to open the Favorites Center; then click the **History** tab. A list of pages you have visited, sorted by date, appears. Simply click a page in the list to open it in the browser window.

Chapter 9

Getting Organized with Your Laptop

Windows Live Mail, which you downloaded in Chapter 3, offers simple Contacts and Calendar tools for keeping track of your contacts and appointments. Perhaps a better option, however, is to use the more robust Windows Live Contacts and Windows Live Calendar, covered in this chapter. Both are offered free of charge from Microsoft's Windows Live Web site.

To use these tools, you must set up a Windows Live account. (Refer to Chapter 3 for help.) After you do, simply direct your Web browser to the Windows Live Web site (http://home.live.com) and log in.

Import Contacts into Windows Live Contacts

Windows Live Contacts stores contact information you enter about people and organizations. But what if you have already entered much of that information in another contacts-management program? Fortunately, instead of requiring you to re-enter that information by hand, Windows Live Contacts enables you to import it. Windows Live Contacts can import contacts from Microsoft Outlook

(covered here), Outlook Express, Windows Contacts, Windows Live Hotmail, Yahoo! Mail, Gmail, and more.

Before you can import contact information, you may need to export it from your current program. The precise steps for this differ depending on the type of program you use. For details, see your program's help information.

Import Contacts into Windows Live Contacts

1 In the main Windows Live Contacts screen, click **Manage**.

Note: To display the main Windows Live Contacts screen, position your mouse pointer over the **Windows Live** link in the upper-right corner of the main Windows Live screen, click **All Services**, and click **Contacts**.

2 Click **Import**.

The Add people screen appears.

3 In the Add people from other services section, click an e-mail service.

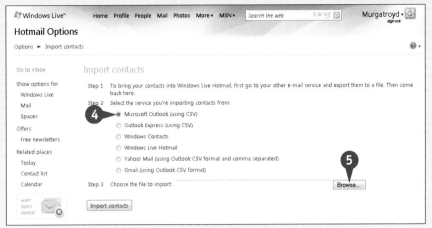

The Import Contacts screen appears.

④ Click the option button next to your old contacts-management program.

⑤ Click **Browse**.

The Choose File to Upload dialog box opens.

⑥ Locate and select the file containing the contacts you want to import.

⑦ Click **Open**.

⑧ Click **Import contacts**.

Windows Live Contacts imports your contacts. To view your contacts, click **Return to contacts**.

Can you sort contacts by last name?
Yes. By default, contacts are listed alphabetically by first name, but you can sort them by last name if you prefer. To do so, click **Options** in the upper-right corner of the screen, click **More Options**, and then click **Display Contacts As...** under Customize Your Contacts. Then click the **Last, First** option button (⊙) and click **Save**.

How do you delete a contact entry?
At times, certain contact entries may need to be deleted. To delete a contact entry, click the check box next to the contact in the main Windows Live Contacts screen, and then click the **Delete** link. When Windows Live Contacts prompts you to confirm the deletion, click **Yes**.

Add a Contact

In addition to importing contacts from other programs, you can add new contacts as needed. When you do, you can include as much or as little information about that contact as you like. For some contacts, including a name and an e-mail address may suffice; for others, you might include additional information, such as the contact's work address, fax number, and so on.

To help manage your contacts, you can organize them into categories. For example, you might put all your contacts from one company in a category. Then, you can quickly view all your contacts from that company as a group.

Add a Contact

1 In the main Windows Live Contacts screen, click **New**.

Note: To display the main Windows Live Contacts screen, position your mouse pointer over the **Windows Live** link in the upper-right corner of the main Windows Live screen, click **All Services**, and click **Contacts**.

2 Under Contact info, enter the contact's first name, last name, nickname, and birthday.

3 Enter the contact's personal e-mail address, home phone number, personal mobile phone number, and home address.

Work info

Company:	Dubois Enterprises ◄ 4
Job Title:	
Work e-mail:	kateshoup@duboisenterprises.com
Work phone:	3175553456
Pager:	
Fax:	
Work address:	1126 Dubois Way
City:	Indianapolis
State/Province:	IN
ZIP/Postal code:	46220
Country:	USA

5 Save   Cancel

Windows Live™   Hotmail (19)   Messenger   Office   Photos | MSN

Kate Shoup

You're friends with Kate. See what you're sharing with each other.

Profile
Details
Photos
Photos of Kate
Documents

Contact info
kateshoup@live.com
(W) kateshoup@duboi...
(H) 3175551234
(M) 3175552345
(W) 3175553456
View all

all in!
Check it out

Edit   Delete   Manage ▾   Categories ▾

◢ Contact info

Name:	Kate Shoup ☆
Nickname:	Kate Shoup
Phone:	3175551234 (H) 3175552345 (M) 3175553456 (W) 3175550123
Fax:	3175554567 (H)
E-mail:	kateshoup@live.com kateshoup@duboisenterprises.com (W) kateshoup@att.net
Address:	6043 Napinou Way Indianapolis, IN 46220 USA (H) 1126 Dubois Way Indianapolis, IN 46220 USA (W)
Notes:	Spouse's Name: Francois

◢ Personal info

Birthday:	May 10, 1972 (38 yrs)

◢ Work and education

4 Under Work info, type the contact's company, work e-mail address, work phone number, pager number, fax number, and work address.

5 Click **Save**.

Windows Live Contacts saves your contact.

How do you categorize a contact?
Before you can apply a category to a contact, you must create the category. To do so, click **Categories** in the main Windows Live Contacts screen and click **New Category**. The New Category screen opens. Type a name for the new category in the **Name** field and click **Save**. The new category appears in the Manage Categories screen. To add a contact to the category, return to the main Windows Live Contacts screen, click the check box next to the contact you want to categorize, click **Categories**, and then click the desired category.

Find and Open a Contact Entry

Windows Live Contacts organizes contacts alphabetically by first name. One way to locate a contact is to simply click a letter along the top of the main Windows Live Contacts screen to reveal all contacts whose first name starts with that letter; then scroll down to locate the contact you want.

If you have a large number of contacts, however, this method can be time-consuming. Fortunately, Windows Live Contacts includes a search function to enable you to locate the contact you need quickly.

Once you have located a contact entry, you can easily view and open it.

Find and Open a Contact Entry

① Type the contact's name in the Windows Live Contacts **Search** box and press `Enter`.

● Windows Live Contacts displays a list of contact entries that match what you typed.

② Click the contact you want to view.

Windows Live Contacts opens the contact entry.

Edit a Contact

Often, you will need to edit contact entries. For example, if someone gets married and changes her name, or if someone moves or changes jobs, you will need to edit the Windows Live Contacts contact entry for that person.

When you edit a contact entry, you see the same screen as when you add a new contact.

This screen enables you to add or change information such as personal information, business information, and more. As when you add a new contact, you can opt to include as little or as much information as you want when you edit a contact.

Edit a Contact

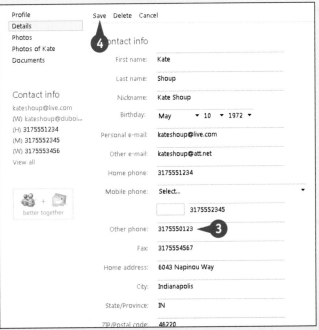

1. Open the contact entry you want to edit.

   Note: For help opening a contact, refer to the preceding section.

2. Click **Edit**.

   *Note: Alternatively, click the check box next to the contact you want to edit in the main Windows Live Contacts window and then click **Edit**.*

   Windows Live Contacts displays the same screen as when you add a new contact.

3. Click in a field and type over the current contents to update them.

4. When you finish editing the contact information, click **Save**.

   Windows Live Contacts saves your changes in the contact entry.

Add an Event to Windows Live Calendar

Windows Live Calendar is a great way to keep track of your schedule. Using Windows Live Calendar, you can plan your daily activities by entering appointments, which Windows Live Calendar calls events. These can be one-time events (such as a lunch date with an old friend) or recurring events (such as a standing meeting) that occur on a daily, weekly, monthly, or yearly basis.

By default, Windows Live Calendar sends you a reminder about an event 15 minutes before it starts, although you can direct Windows Live Calendar to send this reminder minutes, hours, or days in advance.

Add an Event to Windows Live Calendar

1 In the main Windows Live Calendar screen, click **New**.

● The Add an event screen appears.

2 Type a description of the event in the **What** field.

3 Type the location for the event in the **Where** field.

4 Click **Add more details**.

The Windows Live Calendar Event Details screen appears.

5 Click in the leftmost **Start** field and click the date for the event in the calendar that appears.

6 Click in the rightmost **Start** field and click the event's start time in the list that appears.

7 Repeat Steps **5** and **6** in the **End** fields to set the end date and time.

8 If the event is recurring, click **Set recurrence**.

- The Recurrence section expands.

9 Click the **Occurs** ⊡ and click **Daily**, **Weekly**, **Monthly**, or **Yearly**.

Note: What you select in Step 9 affects the remaining options in the Recurrence section.

10 Select additional settings in the Recurrence section.

11 Click the **Send reminder** ⊡ and click the number of minutes, hours, or days before the event the reminder should be sent.

12 Click **Save**.

- Windows Live Calendar adds the event to your calendar.

![Simplify It]

Can you use Windows Live Calendar to invite others to an event?
Yes. To invite others to the event, click **Invite people** in the Event Details screen. In the **To** field that appears, type the invitees' e-mail addresses. When you save the event, Windows Live Calendar asks whether you want to send invitations to the event; if so, click **Send**.

How do you delete an event?
To delete an event — for example, if it is cancelled — position your mouse pointer over the event in Windows Live Calendar and click the **Delete Event** link that appears. If the event is recurring, choose to delete all events in the recurring series or just the selected one. Click **Delete** to confirm the deletion.

Navigate Windows Live Calendar

By default, Windows Live Calendar displays the calendar in Month view. Although this can be handy for getting an overview of your schedule, you cannot view the details of each entry at a glance in this view. Fortunately, Windows Live Calendar enables you to switch to Day view and Week view quickly. It also offers a special Agenda view, which simply lists the day's scheduled events.

Windows Live Calendar also features a thumbnail-sized calendar in the upper-left corner of the screen. You can use this to display a different day, week, or month in the main calendar view.

Navigate Windows Live Calendar

Windows Live Calendar appears in Month view by default.

1 Click the **Week** tab.

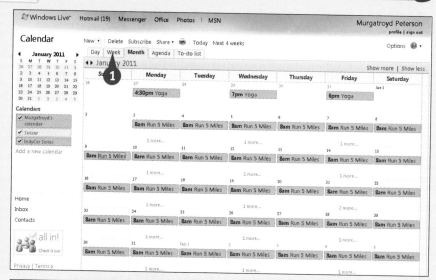

Windows Live Calendar switches to Week view.

2 Click the **Day** tab.

Windows Live Calendar switches to Day view.

③ Click a different day in the thumbnail calendar.

Windows Live Calendar switches to display the day you chose.

④ To view information about an event in your calendar, position your mouse pointer over its entry.

● Windows Live Calendar displays the event's details.

Simplify It

Can you edit an event?
Yes. If the details of an event change — for example, if the event is rescheduled — you can easily edit it. To do so, position your mouse pointer over the event's entry in the calendar and click the **Edit Event** link that appears. If the event is recurring, choose to edit all events in the recurring series or just the selected one. Windows Live Calendar displays the screen you saw when you created the event; click in a field and type over the current contents to update them. Finally, click **Save**. Windows Live Calendar saves your changes to the event.

Create a Calendar

Using Windows Live Calendar, you can create multiple calendars. For example, suppose you coach your child's soccer team, and you need to send the upcoming season's game schedule to the other members of the team. Or maybe you need to share your work schedule with your boss so that she can keep tabs on you. Either way, you can create a new calendar — one for the soccer team, your work schedule, and so on — and add events to it as needed. If you want, you can then share that new calendar with others.

Create a Calendar

1 In the main Windows Live Calendar screen, click the **New** ⊡.

*Note: To display the main Windows Live Calendar screen, position your mouse pointer over the **Windows Live** link in the upper-right corner of the main Windows Live screen, click **All Services**, and click **Calendar**.*

2 Click **Calendar**.

● Alternatively, click **Add a new calendar**.

The Add a new calendar screen appears.

③ Type a name for the calendar in the **Name** field.

④ Click a color tile. Events you create for this calendar appear in this color.

⑤ Type a description.

● If you want to receive a daily e-mail message containing your schedule for the day, click the **Receive a daily e-mail schedule for this calendar** check box (☑) to select it.

⑥ Click **Save**.

● Windows Live Calendar creates the calendar, listing it with your other calendars. Events in this calendar appear in the color you chose.

Simplify It

How do you share a calendar?
To share your calendar, click **Share** in the main Windows Live Calendar window and click the calendar you want to share. The Sharing Settings screen appears. Specify whether you want to share your calendar with friends and family, send friends a view-only link to your calendar, or make your calendar public, and then follow the on-screen prompts. Finally, click **Save**. To stop sharing a calendar, click **Share** in the main Windows Live Calendar screen, click the calendar you no longer want to share, select **Don't Share This Calendar**, click **Save**, and click **Save** again to confirm.

Subscribe to a Calendar

With Windows Live Calendar, you can subscribe to various public calendars, called iCals. For example, if an iCal exists for your favorite sports team, you can subscribe to it; when you do, entries for each game that team plays appears in Windows Live Calendar.

If you know the URL for the iCal to which you want to subscribe, you can initiate the subscription process from within Windows Live Calendar. Alternatively, you can initiate the subscription process from a calendar portal — that is, a Web site offering access to multiple iCals. One such portal is MarkThisDate.com (www.markthisdate.com).

Subscribe to a Calendar

1 In the main Windows Live Calendar screen, click **Subscribe**.

   *Note: To display the main Windows Live Calendar screen, position your mouse pointer over the **Windows Live** link in the upper-right corner of the main Windows Live screen, click **All Services**, and click **Calendar**.*

   The Import or subscribe to a calendar screen appears.

2 Click the **Subscribe to a public calendar** option button (□ changes to ⊙).

3 Type the URL for the iCal to which you want to subscribe in the **Calendar URL** field.

4 Type a name for the iCal in the **Calendar name** field.

5 Click a color tile. Events associated with this calendar appear in this color.

6 Click **Subscribe to calendar**.

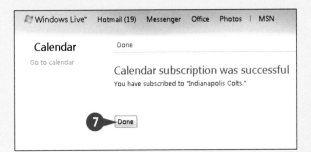

Windows Live Calendar informs you that your subscription was successful.

7 Click **Done**.

● Windows Live Calendar subscribes to the calendar, listing it with your other calendars.

● Windows Live Calendar adds entries contained in the iCal to your calendar, displayed in the color your chose.

How do you add an iCal if the URL is unknown?
You can initiate the subscription process from a calendar portal — that is, a Web site offering access to multiple iCals. One such portal is MarkThisDate.com (www.markthisdate.com). On MarkThisDate.com, locate the iCal you want to download by clicking the appropriate category or using the site's Search box. Then click **Add to Calendar**, and click **Hotmail/Windows Live**. MarkThisDate launches Windows Live Calendar, with the Import or Subscribe to a Calendar screen displayed, the iCal's URL in the Calendar URL field, and the calendar's name in the Calendar Name field. Repeat Steps **5** to **7** of this section to finish the subscription process.

Track To-Do Items

You can use **Windows Live Calendar** to keep a running list of to-do items, or tasks you need to complete. When you enter a to-do item into your To-Do list, you can specify a start time, a deadline, and a priority ranking for the to-do item. If you want, you can direct Windows Live Calendar to send you reminders about any to-do items you enter. You can also enter notes about the to-do item — for example, you might list other people who are involved in completing the item or other details about it. When you complete a to-do item, simply mark it as complete.

Track To-Do Items

1 In the main Windows Live Calendar screen, click the **New** ▾.

> **Note:** To display the main Windows Live Calendar screen, click **More** along the top of the main Windows Live screen and click **Calendar**.

2 Click **To-do**.

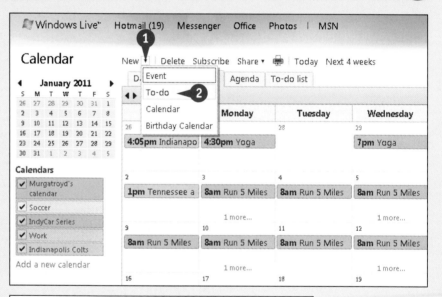

The Add a to-do screen appears.

3 Type a description of the to-do item in the **What** field.

4 Click in the left **Due date** field and click the date on which the to-do item is due.

5 Click in the right **Due date** field and click the time at which the to-do item is due.

6 Click the **Priority** ▾ and a priority level.

7 Click **Add more details**.

The Add a to-do screen expands.

⑧ Click the **Status** ⊡ and click **Not started**, **In progress**, or **Done**.

⑨ Click the **Send reminder** ⊡ and select the number of minutes, hours, days, or weeks before the to-do item is due that the reminder should be sent.

⑩ Type any notes about the to-do item in the Description field.

⑪ Click **Save**.

Windows Live Calendar adds the to-do item to your calendar.

⑫ Click the **To-do list** tab.

● To mark an item as complete, click the ⊡ next to its current status and click **Done**; Windows Live Calendar moves the to-do item to the Done section of the to-do list.

● To delete a to-do item, click its **Delete This To-Do** button (⊠).

Simplify It

Are there other ways to keep track of tasks you need to complete?
Yes. You can use the Windows 7 StickyNotes feature to keep track of tasks you need to complete. These digital notes act like their paper-based brethren, sticking to your computer desktop. To use StickyNotes, click the **Start** button (🔵), click **All Programs**, click **Accessories**, and then click **StickyNotes**. A StickyNote appears on the desktop. Simply click in the StickyNote and type your reminder. When you no longer need your reminder, you can delete your StickyNote. To do so, click the note's **Delete Note** button (⊠). The Delete Note dialog box appears, asking you to confirm the deletion. Click **Yes**.

Chapter 10

Staying in Touch

For many, the primary purpose of a laptop is to keep in touch with others — friends, family members, business associates. One way to do this is via e-mail; others are instant messaging (IM) and video chat.

In Chapter 3, you learned how to download Windows Live Mail, an e-mail program available free of charge from Microsoft's Windows Live Web site. Using Windows Live Mail, you can send, receive, and organize e-mail messages. In Chapter 3, you also learned how to download Windows Live Messenger, a program that you can use to send instant messages and to video-chat.

Compose and Send an E-mail Message

You can use Windows Live Mail to compose and send e-mail messages. Before you do, however, you must sign up with an Internet service provider (ISP) and set up an e-mail address either with that provider or with some other source (such as Hotmail). You must also set up your account within Windows Live Mail using the username and password you established with your e-mail provider. For more details on setting up Windows Live Mail, refer to the program's help information. You can start Windows Live Mail by clicking the program's icon in the Start menu.

Compose and Send an E-mail Message

1 Click **New**.

A New Message window opens.

2 Click in the **To** field and type the recipient's e-mail address.

Note: Windows Live Mail uses Windows Live Contacts as its address book. As you type, Windows Live Mail displays a list of contacts entered in Windows Live Contacts that match what you type. If an entry for the message recipient appears in the list, you can click it to add it to the To field.

3 Optionally, repeat Step **2** to add more recipients to the To field.

4 Click in the **Subject** field and type a subject for your message.

⑤ Click in the main message area and type your message.

⑥ Click **Send**.

Windows Live Mail sends the message to the contact or contacts listed in the To field.

Note: *If you are not connected to the Internet when you click Send, Windows Live Mail saves your message in the Outbox folder. The next time you are connected, you can send the saved message by clicking the* ***Sync*** *button.*

● Windows Live Mail moves a copy of your message to the Sent Items folder.

Simplify It

Is etiquette a concern with e-mail?
Yes. You should avoid sending e-mail messages when angry. Also, keep things short. Your subject line and the body of your message should be clear, concise, and to the point. Finally, use the Windows Live Mail spell-checker. To do so, click the **Check Spelling** button (🔤) in the message window's formatting toolbar.

How do the Windows Live Mail Calendar and Contacts work?
Windows Live Mail also includes simple Contacts and Calendar tools that synchronize with their more robust online counterparts, Windows Live Contacts and Windows Live Calendar, covered in Chapter 9. You can enter contacts and events either from within these Windows Live Mail tools or by using their online equivalents.

Attach a File to an E-mail Message

There may be times when you want to send attachments in your e-mail messages — that is, files you have saved on your computer's hard drive. For example, you might want to e-mail a document containing your resume to apply for a job, or you might want to e-mail a

PowerPoint presentation to a coworker for his or her review. When the recipient receives your message containing the attachment, that person can open and view the attached file on his or her computer (provided he or she has the necessary software installed to read the file).

Attach a File to an E-mail Message

1 In a New Message window, click **Attach**.

● Windows Live Mail launches an Open dialog box.

2 Locate and select the file you want to attach.

3 Click **Open**.

● An entry for the attached file appears under the message's Subject line.

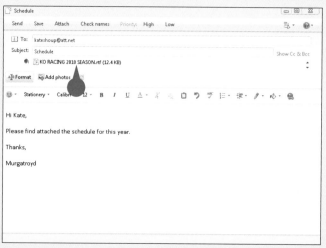

Save a Message as a Draft

Suppose you are writing an important e-mail message — for example, a lengthy e-mail about a legal matter or perhaps a personal e-mail sharing the details of a recent vacation with friends — but do not have time to finish it during the current session. If so, you can save the message as a draft. Messages saved in this manner are stored in the Windows Live Mail Drafts folder, one of several predefined folders in Windows Live Mail. When you are ready to work on the e-mail again, you can access it from the Drafts folder.

Save a Message as a Draft

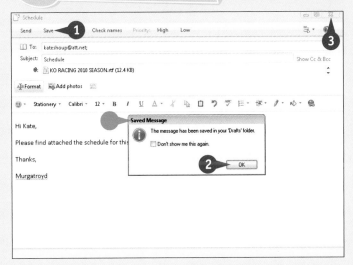

1 In a New Message window, click **Save**.

● The Saved Message dialog box opens, indicating where the message has been saved.

2 Click **OK**.

3 Click the message window's **Close** button (☒).

4 When you are ready to work on the message again, click the **Drafts** folder.

5 Double-click the message in the File list to open it.

Preview and Open Messages

By default, Windows Live Mail downloads new messages anytime you start the program and at 30-minute intervals, while the program is running (assuming your laptop is connected to the Internet). When you receive an e-mail message, an entry for that message appears in the File list of the Inbox folder, with unread messages appearing in bold. You can preview the message's contents in the Windows Live Mail Preview pane or open it in its own message window. If the message contains an attachment, you can open it directly from Windows Live Mail or save it to your hard drive.

Preview and Open Messages

1 Click the **Inbox** folder.

Windows Live Mail displays the Inbox folder's File list.

● New messages appear in bold.

2 Click a message in the File list.

● The message's contents appear in the Preview pane.

3 Double-click the message in the File list.

The message opens in its own window.

● If the e-mail's sender is not in your Windows Live Mail contacts, an Add Contact link appears. Click it to open an Edit Contact dialog box, where you can add info as needed.

● A paperclip icon indicates that the message contains an attachment — that is, a file appended to the message.

4 Right-click the attachment.

5 Click **Open**.

Note: To save rather than open an attachment, click **Save As** instead of Open. Windows Live Mail launches the Save Attachment As dialog box; locate and select the folder in which you want to save the attachment and click **Save**.

Note: Be aware that attachments are known carriers of viruses. Open attachments only if they have been sent by a trusted source.

● The file opens.

Do you have to wait for Windows Live Mail to run its automatic check for mail?
No. To check for mail manually, click the **Sync** ▾ and click which accounts you want to check. (Click **Everything** to also sync Windows Live Mail with Windows Live Calendar and Windows Live Contacts.) Windows Live Mail retrieves any new messages and sends any messages currently in the Outbox folder.

Can you change the automatic-check interval?
Yes. Click the **Menus** button (▤) in the Windows Live Mail toolbar and click **Options**. The Options dialog box opens; in the **General** tab, make sure the **Check for new messages every x minute(s)** check box is selected, and enter a number between 1 and 480 in the spin box. Then click **OK**.

Reply to a Message

It is not unusual to receive a message for which you want to send a reply. With Windows Live Mail, you can quickly and easily reply to any message you receive.

Sometimes, you will receive messages that were also sent to others. If the message to which you are replying was sent to multiple people,

you can reply to the sender only; alternatively, you can choose to reply to the sender as well as to the other recipients.

You can reply to a message from the message window or from the Windows Live Mail Preview pane.

Reply to a Message

① Open the message to which you want to reply.

Note: *You can also simply preview the message in the Windows Live Mail Preview pane.*

② To reply to the sender only, click **Reply**.

● Alternatively, to reply to the sender and to all other recipients of the original message, click **Reply all**.

A new message window opens with the original message text.

● The original subject is preceded with Re:.

● The e-mail address of the original sender (and, if you clicked Reply all, the e-mail addresses of the other recipients of the original message) appears in the To field.

③ Type your reply.

④ Click **Send**.

Windows Live Mail sends your reply.

Forward
a Message

Often, you will receive e-mail messages that you want to forward to others. For example, you might receive a positive e-mail message from your supervisor that you feel should be shared with other members of your team. Or you might receive an amusing e-mail message

from a friend that you want to forward to a mutual acquaintance. Windows Live Mail makes it easy to forward e-mail messages, either from the message window or from the Windows Live Mail Preview pane. You can also add your own text to the forwarded message if desired.

Forward a Message

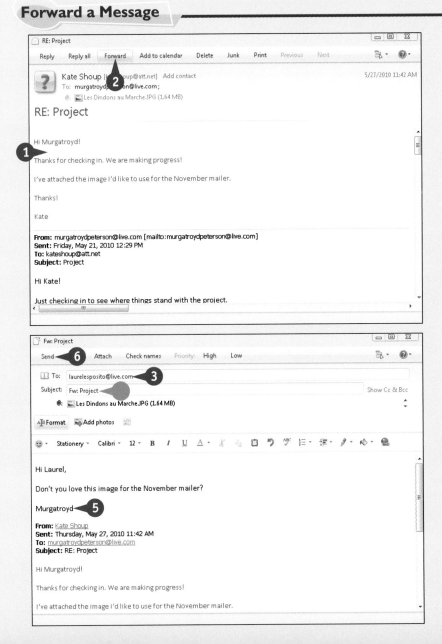

1 Open the message you want to forward.

Note: *Alternatively, preview the message in the Windows Live Mail Preview pane.*

2 Click **Forward**.

A new message window opens with the original message text.

● The original subject is preceded with **Fw**.

3 Click in the **To** field and type the recipient's e-mail address.

Note: *As you type, Windows Live Mail displays contacts entered in Windows Live Contacts that match. If the message recipient's name appears in the list, click it to add it to the To field.*

4 Optionally, repeat Step **3** add more recipients.

5 Type any text you want to add to the forwarded message.

6 Click **Send**.

Windows Live Mail forwards the message.

Save a Message in a Folder

Suppose you frequently receive e-mail messages from the same person. Or perhaps you receive a large number of messages regarding a project you are working on. If so, you can create a folder for storing those messages and give that folder a descriptive name. Folders you create are added to the Windows Live Mail folder list and appear in alphabetical order. After you create the folder, you can move relevant e-mail messages from your e-mail inbox into that folder, much the way you file papers in manila file folders to keep them organized.

Save a Message in a Folder

Create a Folder

1 In the main Windows Live Mail window, click the **New** ⊡.

2 Click **Folder** from the menu that appears.

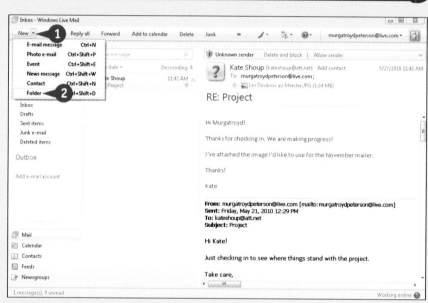

Windows Live Mail launches the Create Folder dialog box.

3 Type a name for the folder in the **Folder name** field.

4 Click the folder in which the new folder should reside.

5 Click **OK**.

● Windows Live Mail creates the new folder, placing it in the folder list.

File a Message in a Folder

① Right-click the message you want to file.

② Click **Move to folder**.

Windows Live Mail launches the Move dialog box.

③ Click the folder to which you want to move the message.

④ Click **OK**.

Windows Live Mail moves the message to the folder you chose.

Is there a faster way to file a message in a folder?	**Can you delete a folder?**
Yes. An even faster way to file an e-mail message is to simply drag it from the File list to the folder list, over the folder to which you want to move it. To copy, rather than move, a message to a folder, press and hold **Ctrl** as you drag the file to the desired folder.	Yes. To delete a folder, right-click it and click **Delete** from the menu that appears. Windows Live Mail prompts you to confirm the deletion; click **Yes**. Note that when you delete a folder, you delete the e-mail messages within that folder.

Find a Message

Even if you carefully file your e-mail messages in folders, messages can still get lost, especially as the number of e-mail messages you receive grows. For example, they can be misfiled. Even messages not misfiled can be difficult to locate if stored in a folder containing a large number of e-mails.

Fortunately, if you have misplaced an e-mail message, you can use Windows Live Mail's Search tool to find it quickly. You can use this tool to locate messages using various criteria, including sender, e-mail address, specific keywords, or anything else you remember about the message.

Find a Message

1 Click the folder in which you want to search.

2 Click in the **Find a Message** field.

3 Type your criteria.

● As you type, Windows Live Mail displays messages that match your criteria.

4 When you see the message you want, click it to preview it in the Preview pane or double-click it to open it in its own window.

Note: If Windows Live Mail fails to locate a match, it displays a **Try searching again in all e-mail** link. Click it to expand your search.

178

Delete a Message

If, after reading a message, you determine that you do not need to keep it for later reference, you can delete it. Deleting unwanted messages is a good way to keep your inbox organized.

Be aware that deleting a message does not completely erase it from your laptop. Instead,

Windows Live Mail moves the message to the Deleted Items folder. If you determine that you have deleted the message in error, you can restore it to its original location. To permanently delete the message, you must empty the Deleted Items folder.

Delete a Message

1 Open the message you want to delete.

Note: *You can also simply preview the message in the Windows Live Mail Preview pane.*

2 Click **Delete**.

The message is moved to the Deleted Items folder.

Note: *To un-delete a message, drag it from the Deleted Items File list to the desired folder.*

3 To permanently delete the message, click the **Deleted items** folder.

4 Click the **Empty This Folder** icon (⊠).

● Windows Live Mail prompts you to confirm the deletion.

5 Click **Yes**.

The contents of the Deleted Items folder are permanently deleted.

Add a Contact to Windows Live Messenger

Windows Live Messenger is an instant-messaging (IM) program that you can download free from the Microsoft Windows Live Web site. (To download this program, see Chapter 3.) You can start Windows Live Messenger by clicking its icon in the Start menu. After you start Windows Live Messenger, you log on using your Windows Live ID.

Before you can communicate with someone using Windows Live Messenger, you must add that person as a Windows Live Messenger contact, and invite him or her to chat online with you.

Add a Contact to Windows Live Messenger

1 In the Windows Live Messenger window, click the **Add a contact or group** button (⊞).

2 Click **Add a contact**.

A Windows Live Messenger dialog box appears.

3 Type the person's IM address in the **Instant messaging address** field.

4 Click **Next**.

5 Type a message to the person you want to invite to chat in the **Include your own message (optional)** field.

6 Click **Send invitation**.

Windows Live Messenger informs you that you have added the person to your contacts, and that as soon as he or she accepts your invitation, you can chat.

7 Click **Close**.

How do you add a picture to the Windows Live Messenger profile?
Click the ⬇ next to your screen name and click **Change Display Picture**. In the dialog box that opens, choose from the available images or click **Browse** to select an image stored on your hard drive. Then click **OK**.

Start a New IM Thread

When a contact you have set up in Windows Live Messenger is online, logged in to the service, and available to chat, that person's name appears in your Windows Live Messenger Available list. If you want, you can send that person an instant message, starting a new IM thread.

Windows Live Messenger includes several visual tools for expressing yourself during your IM sessions. For example, you can include emoticons in your messages — small icons that convey a facial expression or other idea. This can help ensure that the true meaning of your message is conveyed.

Start a New IM Thread

1 Right-click the person you want to IM.

2 Click **Send an instant message**.

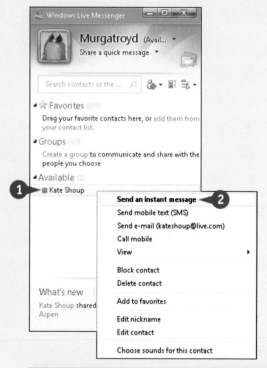

A Windows Live Messenger window opens.

3 Type your message and press Enter.

Design your Future Baby!

Make a Baby! Combine pics to...

● The person's reply appears in the Windows Live Messenger window.

④ Type additional IMs as desired.

⑤ To add an emoticon to an IM, click the **Select an Emoticon** button (🙂).

Note: In addition to emoticons, Windows Live Messenger supports winks, which are animated greetings you can send to your contacts, and nudges, which cause the conversation window to vibrate.

⑥ Click the desired emoticon from the list that appears.

Can you change the sound settings?
Yes. To change the sound that plays when someone sends you an IM, right-click the person's name in the Windows Live Messenger window and select **Choose sounds for this contact**. Then, under Sends you an instant message, select the sound you want to hear. Finally, click **OK**.

Receive and Respond to an IM

If Windows Live Messenger is running on your laptop and you are signed in to the service, you can receive IMs in real time from your Windows Live Messenger contacts. When you do, you receive both a visual alert in the taskbar's notification area as well as an auditory alert.

(As you learned in the preceding section, you can change the sound played when you receive an IM.) When you receive an IM, you can easily respond to it, thereby engaging in a text-based conversation in real time.

Receive and Respond to an IM

● When you receive an IM, a visual alert appears in the taskbar's notification area.

1 Click the alert.

A Windows Live Messenger window opens.

2 Type your reply and press Enter.

Share a Photo

In addition to using Windows Live Messenger to conduct text-based conversations in real time, you can use the service to quickly and easily share a photo at any time in an IM thread. For example, you might share a photo of a new pet, a mutual friend, a funny sign — really, anything. Note that Windows Live Messenger can only support sharing of photos in JPEG, GIF, BMP, or PNG format. When you share a photo with someone else, that person has the option to save it to his or her hard drive.

Share a Photo

1 During an IM thread, click **Photos** in the Windows Live Messenger window.

● A Select Images to Start Sharing dialog box opens.

2 Locate and select the photo you want to share.

3 Click **Open**.

● The photo is added to the IM thread.

● To save a photo in an IM thread, position your mouse pointer over the photo and click the **Save** button (▣) that appears.

Set Up Video Calling

In addition to simple text-based conversations, Windows Live Messenger can be used to place video calls. To use Windows Live Messenger for this purpose, your laptop must feature a webcam, a microphone and speakers (a headset is recommended), a broadband Internet connection, and a full-duplex sound card. (With a full-duplex sound card, two people can speak simultaneously.) Also, the person you want to call should be similarly equipped. Note that the quality of the audio and video may vary depending on your hardware and Internet connection speed. Before you can place your first video call, you must set up this feature.

Set Up Video Calling

1 Click the **Show Menu** button (▣▾).

2 Click **Tools**.

3 Click **Audio and video setup**.

The Set Up Audio and Video – Speaker/Microphone or Speakerphone dialog box opens.

4 Click the **Select the speaker/ microphone or speakerphone you want to use** ▾ and select click **Custom**.

5 Click the **Speaker** ▾ and select click the speaker you want to use.

6 Click **Test** to test the speakers. You should hear a series of notes play back.

Note: *When you click the Test button, it toggles to a Stop button. Click **Stop** to stop playing back the series of notes.*

⑦ Click the **Microphone** ▾ and select the microphone you want to use.

⑧ Speak into the microphone.

● As you speak, an indicator appears, reflecting the level of your voice.

⑨ Click **Next**.

The Set Up Audio and Video – Webcam dialog box opens.

⑩ Click the **Select the webcam you want to use to place video calls** ▾ and select the webcam you want to use.

● A preview of the webcam feed appears.

⑪ Click **Finish**.

How do you change webcam settings?
To adjust webcam settings, click the **Webcam Settings** button in the Set Up Audio and Video – Webcam dialog box. A Properties dialog box opens, offering settings for adjusting the brightness, contrast, hue, sharpness, exposure, white balance, and more.

Place a Video Call

As mentioned, in addition to using Windows Live Messenger to conduct simple text-based conversations, you can use the service for video calling, assuming your laptop (and the computer of the person with whom you want to speak) has been set up for the job, as covered in the preceding task.

When you place a video call, Windows Live Messenger prompts the call recipient to accept your call. When he or she does, you can commence speaking, and you will be able to see him or her on your laptop screen. You end the call with the simple click of a link.

Place a Video Call

① Click the **Show Menu** button (▣▾).

② Click **Actions**.

③ Click **Video**.

④ Click **Start a Video Call**.

The Select a Contact dialog box opens.

⑤ Click the contact you want to call.

● The contact's name appears in the list at the bottom.

⑥ Click **OK**.

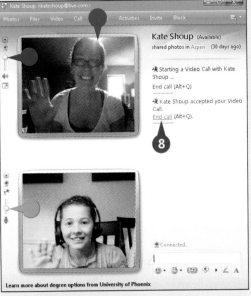

Windows Live Messenger starts a video call and invites the selected contact to join in.

● The feed from your webcam is visible in the Windows Live Messenger screen.

● When the recipient accepts the call, the feed from his or her webcam appears in the Windows Live Messenger screen.

7 Commence speaking as normal.

● Click and drag the volume slider by your webcam feed to adjust your mic volume.

● Click and drag the volume slider by your conversation partner's webcam feed to adjust the speaker volume.

8 To end the call, click **End call**.

Simplify It

How do you switch to full-screen view?
To switch to full-screen view, click the **Switch to Full-Screen View** button (□) next to your conversation partner's Web feed. Your conversation partner's Web feed covers the screen, and a small window with your Web feed appears in the lower-right corner. To revert to regular view, click the ◪ button in the upper-right corner of the screen.

How do you accept an incoming video call?
When someone is attempting to contact you via video call, an alert appears in your taskbar's notification area, just as if you were receiving a regular IM. Click **Accept** in the alert. Alternatively, decline the call by clicking **Decline**.

Chapter 11

Networking Your Laptop PC

A network consists of any group of connected computers. Networks enable collaboration through sharing of files, equipment (such as printers), and Internet connections.

There are several types of networks. For example, Ethernet networks use special cables to transmit information; HomePNA networks relay data via existing telephone wires; and powerline networks use existing electrical wires to transmit information.

There are also wireless networks, which in addition to being the easiest type of network to set up, offer laptop users the most mobility because they transmit information via radio waves rather than wires or cables. Using your laptop with a wireless network is the focus of this chapter.

Set Up a Wireless Network

Setting up a wireless network is simple — if you have all the necessary components. Specifically, each computer you want to connect to the network needs a wireless card, also called a network adapter. (Most laptops come with wireless cards preinstalled.)

In addition, you need a wireless router, which connects computers and transmits information between them via radio signals. Certain routers are designed to work seamlessly with Windows 7; a feature called Windows Connect Now (WCN) enables you to set them up automatically, as shown here.

Securing your network is critical; otherwise, outsiders may be able to access information shared on your network

Set Up the Router

1 Plug the router into a power outlet.

> *Note: You should locate your router such that the computers on your network receive the strongest signal with the least amount of interference. Opt for a central location — as close to the center of your home or office as possible. Also, position it off the floor and away from walls and from metal objects such as filing cabinets.*

2 Click the **Wireless Networks** icon (▣) in the taskbar's notification area.

● Windows 7 displays a list of available networks, including an entry for your router (identified by the manufacturer name).

> *Note: If your router is not WCN-compliant, use the setup CD that came with the router to set it up manually. For more information, see the Windows 7 Help article titled "Set Up a Wireless Router."*

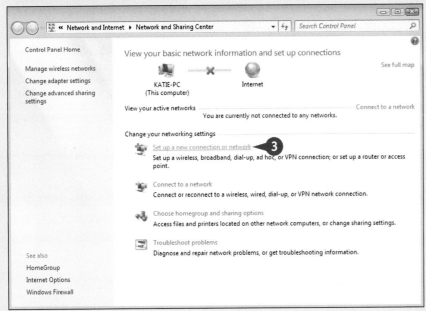

Secure the Router

1 Click the **Wireless Networks** icon () in the taskbar's notification area.

2 Click **Open Network and Sharing Center**.

3 Under Change your networking settings, click **Set up a new connection or network**.

How do you connect your network to the Internet?
If you want the computers on your wireless network to be able to access the Internet via a shared connection, you need an Internet connection — preferably of the broadband variety (cable or DSL). You obtain an Internet connection and the necessary equipment from an Internet service provider (ISP). To connect your network to the Internet, plug one end of an Ethernet cable into the Internet port on your router and the other end into your broadband modem; then connect the cable supplied by your broadband provider from the appropriate wall outlet to your modem.

continued

Set Up a Wireless Network *(continued)*

When securing your wireless network, you should select a passphrase or security key that will be difficult for others to guess, but that you will be sure to remember. Choose a mixture of numbers with uppercase and lowercase letters, and avoid strings of characters that compose identifiable words, names, or dates. If

need be, write down your security key or passphrase and store it in a safe place.

In addition to setting a security key or passphrase, you should install a firewall on each computer on your network to protect the network from hackers and malicious software. You learn how to install a firewall in Chapter 13.

Set Up a Wireless Network *(continued)*

Secure the Router (continued)

Windows 7 launches the Set Up a Connection or Network Wizard.

④ Click **Set up a new network**.

⑤ Click **Next**.

⑥ Click the router you want to configure.

⑦ Click **Next**.

Set Up a Network

To set up a network, type the 8-digit PIN from the router label

You can find the numeric PIN on a label attached to the router or in the printed information that came from the manufacturer.

PIN: 26822682 ◄ 8

9 ► Next   Cancel

Set Up a Network

Give your network a name

Your network needs a unique name so that it can be easily identified. It is best to keep the name short (25 characters or less) and recognizable.

Type your network name:
Lapin ◄ 10

Security-enabled network
Your network is being set up using WPA2-Personal.

Change passphrase, security level and encryption type (advanced):

Security key:
£d6043k s6039 ◄ 11

☑ Connect automatically

Security level:
WPA2-Personal (Recommended)

Encryption type:
AES (Recommended)

🛡 Upgrade or replace the router using the network settings stored on this computer

12 ► Next   Cancel

8 Type the router's PIN (located on the bottom of the router).

9 Click **Next**.

10 Type a name for your network in the **Type your network name** field.

11 Type a security key for your network in the **Security key** field.

Note: *If your network supports the use of WPA2- or WPA-level security, your security key can be a passphrase rather than a cryptic sequence of numbers.*

12 Click **Next**.

Windows 7 applies your changes to the network.

Are there different wireless network technologies?
Yes. There are a few different types of wireless network technologies: 802.11a, 802.11b, 802.11g, and 802.11n, with 802.11g and 802.11n offering the fastest data-transmission speeds and strongest wireless signals. Your wireless card must be compatible with the network technology that your wireless router uses.

What do you do if your network does not work?
If you have a problem with your network, you can troubleshoot it with the Windows 7 Network Troubleshooter. To do so, right-click the **Wireless Networks** icon in the taskbar and select **Troubleshoot Problems**. Then click the entry in the list that best reflects the problem you are experiencing with your network and follow the on-screen prompts.

Connect to a Wireless Network

After you set up your wireless network, you can connect to it with your laptop — assuming your laptop has a wireless card installed.

If your wireless network is connected to the Internet, you can then access the Internet from your laptop. You may also be able to access files other computers are sharing on the wireless network.

In addition to connecting to your own wireless network, you can connect to public wireless networks, often found in airports, hotels, cafes, libraries, and other public places.

Connect to a Wireless Network

1 Click the **Wireless Networks** icon (🖥) in the Windows 7 taskbar's notification area.

A list of wireless networks in your area appears.

2 Click the wireless network you want to use to connect.

A Connect button appears.

3 Click **Connect**.

4 If prompted, enter the network password or network security key.

5 Click **OK**.

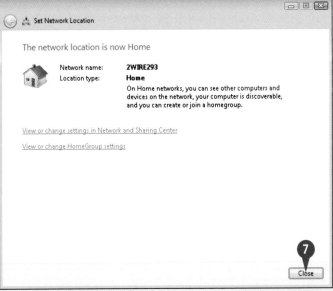

If this is the first time you have connected to this wireless network, Windows 7 prompts you to specify whether it is a home, work, or public network.

⑥ Click **Home network**, **Work network**, or **Public network**.

Windows 7 confirms your selection.

⑦ Click **Close**.

Note: If connecting to a public network, you may need to create an account to log on. To find out, launch your Web browser.

*Note: To disconnect from a wireless network, click the **Wireless Networks** icon (▨) in the Windows 7 taskbar, click the wireless network to which you are connected, and click **Disconnect**.*

How do you know if your laptop has a wireless card installed?
To determine whether your computer features a wireless card, open Windows 7 Device Manager, double-click the **Network Adapters** entry in the list of devices, and look for a device with "wireless" or "WiFi" in its name.

How do you connect to a public wireless network?
You connect to a public network the same way as a private one, but you may have to create an account with the public network provider to log on. To find out, launch your Web browser after connecting to the network; if an account is required, you will be directed to a special Web page where you can create one.

Share Files and Folders via Public Folders

Windows 7 offers special folders, called Public folders, which you can use to share files with other users. There are four Public folders: Public Documents, Public Music, Public Pictures, and Public Videos. These folders are subfolders of the main Documents, Music, Pictures, and Videos folders, respectively.

When you place an item in a Public folder, any other person with a user account on that same computer can view it by default. In addition, you can make these folders accessible to other users whose computers are connected to your network. To do so, you must enable sharing.

Share Files and Folders via Public Folders

① Click the **Wireless Networks** icon (▣) in the taskbar's notification area.

② Click **Open Network and Sharing Center**.

The Network and Sharing Center window opens.

③ Click **Change advanced sharing settings** on the left side of the Network and Sharing Center window.

The Advanced sharing settings window opens.

Note: *An even faster way to open the Advanced sharing settings window is to open one of your Public folders, click* **Share With***, and click* **Advanced Sharing Settings***.*

④ If necessary, click the ⊡ to the right of your current profile to expand it.

⑤ Under Public folder sharing, click the **Turn on sharing...** option (◉) to select it.

⑥ Click **Save changes**.

How do you share a file or folder?
To share a file or folder, simply move or copy it to the relevant Public folder to make it accessible to others. When you do, others can open and work with the file or folder as if it were stored on their own PC.

How do you limit what other users can do with shared items?
To limit what others can do with items you share, you can apply permissions. Permissions are like rules that specify the level of access a user has. For example, you can limit others to simply opening files you share, or you can allow them to modify them, or even create new files in your shared folders. For details, see the Windows 7 Help information.

Set Up a Homegroup

You can share files and folders by creating a homegroup, which other Windows 7 computers on your network can join. When you create or join a group, you specify which of your items you want to share and which should remain private.

To create a homegroup, your network must be a home network, as opposed to a work or public network. You can change from a work or public network to a home network by clicking the Public Network or Work Network link in the Network and Sharing Center window and then clicking Home Network in the screen that appears.

Set Up a Homegroup

1 In the Network and Sharing Center window, next to HomeGroup, click **Ready to create**.

Note: To open the Network and Sharing Center window, click the ***Wireless Networks*** icon (■) in the taskbar's notification area and click ***Open Network and Sharing Center***.

The HomeGroup window opens.

2 Click **Create a homegroup**.

The Create a Homegroup Wizard starts.

③ Click the check box (☑) next to each folder you want to share with the homegroup.

Note: You can also share a printer with your homegroup.

④ Click **Next**.

● The Create a Homegroup Wizard generates a password.

⑤ Write down the password.

Note: You need this password to add other PCs to the homegroup.

⑥ Click **Finish**.

Windows 7 creates the homegroup.

*Note: To add another Windows 7 PC to the homegroup, open the PC's Control Panel and click **Choose Homegroup and Sharing Options** under Network and Internet. Click **Join Now** in the screen that appears and follow the on-screen prompts.*

Simplify It

How do you set up a workgroup?
Only computers running Windows 7 can join a homegroup. If computers on your network are running a different version of Windows, you must use a workgroup instead. Windows creates a workgroup and gives it a name when you set up a network; the problem is, the name of the workgroup may be different depending on what version of Windows you are running. To share files and folders among the various computers on the network, you must ensure that the workgroup name listed for each computer is the same. To find out how, view each computer's help information.

Share Within Your Homegroup

When you set up a homegroup, you specify what top-level folders should be shared. You can also opt to share individual files and subfolders with others.

These resources can be shared with Read permissions, enabling others to simply open and view your files. Alternatively, you can share with Read/Write permissions, enabling others to both view and modify your files. You can share with everyone in your homegroup or with specific individuals. Shared resources appear under Homegroup in the Windows Explorer Navigation pane. Of course, if you change your mind, you can always unshare a resource.

1 In Windows Explorer, locate and select the resource you want to share.

2 Click **Share with**.

3 Click a sharing option.

● Click **Homegroup (Read)** to share the resource with Read permissions with everyone in your homegroup.

● Click **Homegroup (Read/Write)** to share the resource with Read and Write permissions with everyone in your homegroup.

● Click **Specific people** to share the resource with specific people in the homegroup, as shown here.

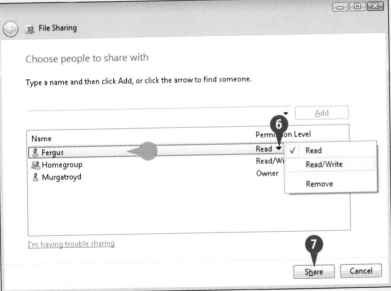

Windows 7 launches the File Sharing Wizard.

④ Type the username of the person with whom you want to share the resource.

⑤ Click **Add**.

Note: *If you are not sure what the person's username is, click the ⊡ to the left of the **Add** button and select the user from the list.*

● Windows 7 adds the selected user to the list of users with access to the resource.

⑥ To set the permission level, click the ⊡ next to the current permission and select **Read** or **Read/Write**.

⑦ Click **Share**.

The resource you selected is shared.

Note: *To stop sharing a resource, right-click the resource you want to keep private, click **Share With**, and select **Nobody**.*

Simplify It

Can you share a printer with a homegroup?
Yes. You can share a printer with other members of your homegroup, who then access the printer through the Print dialog box. To do so, connect the printer to any computer in the homegroup. Then, in that computer's main Control Panel window, click **Choose Homegroup and Sharing Options** under **Network and Internet**. The HomeGroup screen appears; under Share Libraries and Printers, select the **Printers** check box and click **Save Changes**. Next, set up each computer on the homegroup to print by opening its Control Panel window, clicking **Choose Homegroup and Sharing Options**, clicking **Install Printer**, and clicking **Install Driver** if prompted.

Maintaining Your Laptop PC

Periodically performing a bit of housecleaning goes a long way toward keeping your laptop running smoothly. For example, you should regularly ensure that your laptop's Windows 7 operating system has received all the necessary updates from Microsoft, that your files are backed up, that unnecessary files have been deleted in order to free up disk space, that your hard drive is not overly fragmented, that your hard drive is not experiencing errors, and that your laptop screen and keyboard are clean and protected. You access many of the tools needed for system maintenance from the Windows 7 Control Panel.

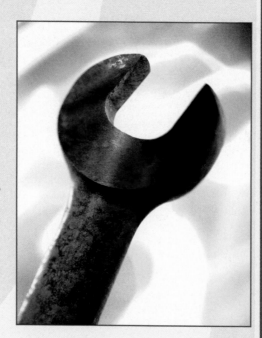

Explore the Windows 7 Control Panel

The Windows 7 Control Panel acts like a master console of sorts. It serves as a launching point for performing many system-maintenance tasks, such as updating your Windows 7 system, backing up your files, freeing disk space, defragmenting your hard drive, and more.

The main Control Panel window features several links. You click a link to access related tools or wizards. If you know the name of the tool you need to access but are not sure which series of links to click to access it, you can use the Control Panel window's Search box to find it.

Explore the Windows 7 Control Panel

1 Click the **Start** button (⊞).

The Start menu opens.

2 Click **Control Panel**.

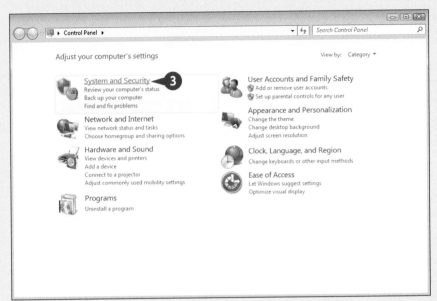

The main Control Panel window opens.

③ Click **System and Security**.

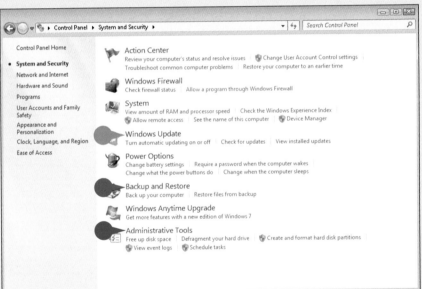

The System and Security window opens.

● Click **Windows Update** to launch the Windows Update tool.

● Click **Backup and Restore** to back up your computer.

● Click **Administrative Tools** to access tools for freeing disk space and defragmenting your hard drive.

Simplify It

How do you find a tool in Control Panel?
If you are not sure what link to click to access a particular tool, you can use the Control Panel window's Search box to find it. Simply type the name of the tool you want to find in the Search box; a list of tools that match what you typed appears.

207

Update Your Windows 7 System

Microsoft regularly releases updates for Windows 7 — that is, changes to the operating system designed to prevent or fix problems or to enhance security or performance.

Windows 7 automatically checks for updates and installs those it deems essential. But there are additional, optional updates that Windows 7 does not automatically install; you should regularly view these updates and install them as needed. You can also perform a manual update if Microsoft has released a new update but your system has not yet run its automatic-update operation. (Note that to download an update, your laptop must be connected to the Internet.)

Update Your Windows 7 System

1 In the Windows Control Panel's System and Security window, click **Windows Update**.

Note: For help accessing the System and Security window, refer to the section "Explore the Windows 7 Control Panel."

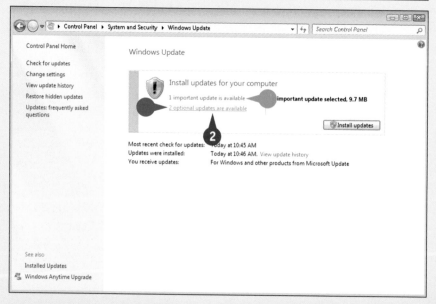

The Windows Update window opens.

● In this case, one important update is available.

● In this case, two optional updates are available.

2 Click the **X optional updates are available** link.

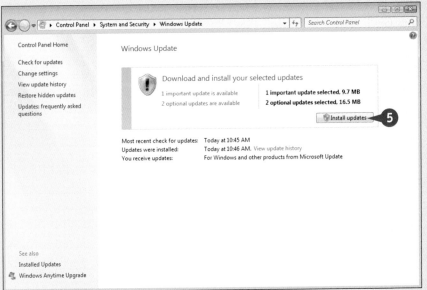

The Select the Updates You Want to Install screen appears.

③ Click the check box (☑) next to any optional updates you want to install to select them.

● You can click **Important** to view the updates Microsoft has deemed essential, which are selected for download by default.

④ Click **OK**.

⑤ Click **Install updates**.

Windows 7 downloads and installs any selected updates and informs you when the operation is complete.

Note: *You may be prompted to restart your computer for the updates to take effect.*

Can you change the automatic-update settings?
Yes. To change the automatic-update settings — for example, change the time of day when Windows 7 performs automatic updates or specify that no updates be installed until you have had the opportunity to review them (recommended if you run specialized programs such as music-production software, which may not interact well with updates) — click **Change settings** along the left side of the Windows Update window. Then, under Important Updates, click the **Install updates automatically (recommended)** ▾ and choose a different option. Click the **Install new updates** ▾ to specify the day(s) and time when updates should run, and after reviewing the remaining options, click **OK**.

Set Up Automatic Backups

If a disaster such as theft, loss, breakage, or virus attack were to befall your computer, certain files, such as digital pictures, would be impossible to replace. Others, such as files used for work, would be at best extremely difficult to reconstruct. For this reason, you should back up your files — that is, copy them to an external hard drive, a Flash drive, a CD, a DVD, or a network resource. Wherever you save your backup, you should keep it in a safe, separate location from your computer. You can run manual backups, or you can set up Windows 7 to perform backups automatically.

Set Up Automatic Backups

1 Connect the drive on which you want to save your backup to your laptop, insert the necessary media, or connect to the appropriate network.

2 In the Control Panel's System and Security window, click **Backup and Restore**.

Note: For help accessing the System and Security window, refer to the section "Explore the Windows 7 Control Panel."

The Backup and Restore window appears.

3 Click **Set up backup**.

● Windows 7 launches the Set Up Backup Wizard.

4 Click the drive on which you want to store the backup.

Note: To save the backup in a folder on the network, click the button and specify the network path and any required username and password information in the screen that appears.

5 Click **Next**.

6 Click **Let Windows choose** to perform a backup on a standard set of folders.

● If you want, you can click **Let me choose** to limit the backup to certain folders.

7 Click **Next**.

8 Review the backup settings.

● To change the backup schedule, click **Change schedule** and make your changes.

9 Click **Save settings and run backup**.

Windows launches the backup operation. Subsequent backups will occur on the schedule specified.

*Note: After you set up Windows Backup, you can run a manual backup — for example, if your automatic backup did not occur as scheduled. Simply click the **Back Up Now** button in the Backup and Restore window.*

How do you restore a backup?
To restore your backed up files and folders in the event of system failure or some other disaster, first attach, insert, or connect to the media on which the backup is stored. Then, in the Backup and Restore window, click **Restore my files**. Windows 7 launches the Restore Files Wizard. To restore all folders and files in your system, click **Browse for folders**, locate the folder containing the backup of your hard drive, click **Add folder**, and click **Next**. Then click **In the original location** and click **Restore**. Windows 7 restores the files and notifies you when the restore operation is complete; click **Finish**.

Delete Unnecessary Files

In addition to storing files you create or save as you work on your computer, your laptop's hard drive stores many more files that Windows 7 creates, changes, and saves automatically. Over time, you can end up with a gigabyte or more of unneeded files, consuming valuable space on your hard drive.

If your hard drive is low on free space, you can use the Disk Cleanup tool to find and remove these temporary files. This utility also empties the Recycle Bin. In fact, it is wise to run the Disk Cleanup tool regularly as part of standard disk management.

Delete Unnecessary Files

1 In the Control Panel's System and Security window, under Administrative Tools, click **Free up disk space**.

Note: For help accessing the System and Security window, refer to the section "Explore the Windows 7 Control Panel."

● The Disk Cleanup: Drive Selection dialog box appears.

2 Click the **Drives** ⊡ and select the drive you want to clean.

3 Click **OK**.

Disk Cleanup scans your system to determine how much space can be freed.

When the scan is complete, the Disk Cleanup dialog box opens.

④ Click the check box (☑) next to each type of file you want to delete.

⑤ Click **OK**.

Disk Cleanup prompts you to confirm the cleanup operation.

⑥ Click **Delete Files**.

Disk Cleanup deletes the unnecessary files, freeing up disk space.

Simplify It

How do you check the free space on your hard drive?
To quickly view the amount of free space on your hard drive, click the **Start** button and click **Computer**. The Computer window opens; click the disk you want to check to view the size of the drive and the available space. To view additional information about the drive, right-click its icon and click **Properties**.

How can you find out more about the files that Disk Cleanup wants to delete?
To access more details about files that Disk Cleanup wants to delete, click **View Files** in the Disk Cleanup dialog box. These details include the size of the files, when they were created, and when you last accessed them.

Defragment Your Hard Drive

When you save a file on your laptop, Windows 7 writes the data to a sector on the hard drive. If the sector is too small to hold the entire file, the extra bits are saved in the next available sector.

Over time, your files may become quite fragmented, with bits spread across several

sectors on the drive, meaning when you open a file, it takes Windows longer to find all the various pieces. To solve this problem, you can run Disk Defragmenter. This reassembles the files on your hard drive such that each one occupies as few sectors as possible.

Defragment Your Hard Drive

1 In the Control Panel's System and Security window, under Administrative Tools, click **Defragment your hard drive**.

Note: For help accessing the System and Security window, refer to the section "Explore the Windows 7 Control Panel."

Windows 7 launches the Disk Defragmenter utility.

2 Click the drive you want to defragment.

● Before defragmenting a drive, you can click **Analyze disk** to determine how fragmented it is.

3 To defragment the disk, click **Defragment disk**.

● Disk Defragmenter analyzes the disk.

Disk Defragmenter defragments the disk. Note that the process can take several minutes or longer.

● When the operation is complete, the drive is shown as 0% fragmented.

④ Click **Close**.

Simplify It

Can you set up Windows 7 to defragment automatically?
Yes. Click **Configure schedule** in the Disk Defragmenter window. Then, in the Disk Defragmenter: Modify Schedule dialog box, select the **Run on a schedule** check box and set the frequency with which Disk Defragmenter should run. Next, click **Select disks**. Click the disks you want to defragment, click **OK**, and click **OK** again.

Check Your Hard Drive for Errors

Problems with your hard drive can cause files to become corrupted. This can prevent you from running a program or opening a document. You can set up Windows 7's Check Disk program to look for and fix hard-drive errors. Then, next time you restart your computer, Windows 7 performs a check.

Check Disk runs two different types of checks: a basic hard-drive check and a more thorough bad-sector check. (A bad sector is one that can no longer reliably store data.) You should perform the basic check about once a week; perform the more thorough bad-sector check once a month.

Check Your Hard Drive for Errors

1 Click the **Start** button (⊞).

2 Click **Computer**.

The Computer folder window opens.

3 Right-click the disk you want to check.

4 Click **Properties**.

The Properties dialog box opens.

5 Click the **Tools** tab.

6 Click **Check now**.

7 To instruct Check Disk to fix any errors it finds, click the **Automatically fix file system errors** option (☑).

● To look for bad sectors, check the **Scan for and attempt recovery of bad sectors** option.

8 Click **Start**.

9 Click **Schedule disk check** to run the check the next time you start your PC.

10 Click the **Start** button (▣).

11 Click the ▣ next to the **Shut down** option.

12 Click **Restart**.

Before restarting your computer, Windows 7 runs the Disk Check utility.

Simplify It

Can you schedule maintenance tasks to run automatically?
Yes. Windows 7 includes a utility called Task Scheduler, which you can use to run tasks automatically on a schedule you specify. To launch Task Scheduler, open the System and Security window in the Control Panel and click **Schedule tasks** under Administrative Tools. Then create a scheduled task by opening the **Action** menu and clicking **Create Basic Task**. Type a name and description for the task, click **Next**, and specify the schedule on which it should run. Click **Start a Program**, click **Next**, click **Browse** to locate the program you want to launch automatically, click **Next** again, and click **Finish**.

Clean and Protect Your Screen and Keyboard

Laptop screens are typically of the liquid crystal display (LCD) variety. They are somewhat soft to the touch, and can be damaged rather easily. For this reason, you must take care to avoid scratching, poking, denting, or puncturing the screen; otherwise, it may become unusable. Although you can replace a laptop screen, doing so is expensive. For this reason, you should take good care of the laptop screen.

You should also take care of your keyboard. It is a good idea to clean your keyboard periodically to keep keys from becoming stuck or damaged.

Clean the Screen

Use a special microfiber cloth (usually made of polyester and nylon) to dust your screen. To avoid denting or otherwise damaging the screen as you clean it, do not press too hard on the screen with the cloth. If you use a liquid cleaning agent, be sure to remove the battery before cleaning your screen.

Cleaning Agents

Avoid ammonia-based cleaning liquids, such as Windex. These can damage your screen by removing anti-glare and anti-static coatings on the surface. Instead, use isopropyl alcohol. Do not ever spray or pour a cleaner on the monitor surface; instead, coat a cloth or cotton swab with the cleaner and rub that gently on the screen.

Protect Your Screen from Damage

When you are not using your laptop, close the clamshell lid. Consider purchasing a padded bag for your laptop for storing when not in use. Never place sharp objects, such as pens or your fingernail, against the screen. Be aware that exposure to extreme temperatures can cause problems with laptop displays.

Avoid Spills

To avoid damaging your laptop, it is a good idea to avoid eating or drinking around your laptop. You can clean out spilled crumbs of food, but spilled liquids can be disastrous — especially to your keyboard. If you must eat while working on your laptop, try to keep any liquids at a safe distance.

Clean the Keys

You can clean the keys in a few ways. One is to run a handheld mini vacuum along the keys to pick up any dust or crumbs that have fallen in. You can also use a nonabrasive liquid cleaner to clean the surface of the keys. Never apply the cleaner to the actual keyboard, however; instead, spray it on a soft cloth and then wipe the keys with the cloth.

Clean Under the Keys

With some keyboards, you can easily remove the keys by gently popping them off with a screwdriver or coin. You can then use a nonabrasive liquid cleaner to clean underneath them. Again, do not apply the cleaner directly; instead, spray it on a soft cloth, and then use the cloth to clean under the keys. When you are finished cleaning under the keys, you can simply pop the keys back into place.

Replace a Damaged Key

If you break or otherwise damage a key, you may be able to replace it. Laptop keys are made of three components: the key cap, which is the visible portion of the key; a cup, which is a small rubber component, and a hinge, also called a retainer clip. You need all three pieces for the key to function properly. Be aware that removing and replacing larger keys such as the spacebar is slightly more difficult. You should check your owner's manual first to see if your manufacturer recommends replacing a key.

Chapter 13

Securing Your Laptop PC

If your laptop is connected to the Internet, it is vulnerable to any number of threats, including crackers, viruses, spyware, and more. Even an unconnected laptop can be compromised by someone who gains physical access to it.

Fortunately, you can take certain steps to counter these threats. For example, password-protecting your laptop prevents someone who gains physical access to it from logging on. In addition, you can encrypt your data, install a firewall, and filter spam and scams from your e-mail.

You can protect any children who use your laptop by enabling Windows 7 parental controls and Internet Explorer 8's Content Advisor tool.

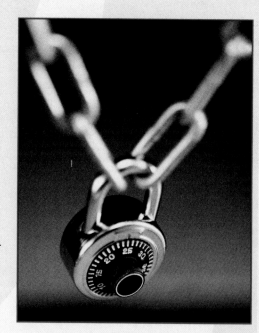

Understanding Computer Security

Using your laptop, especially online, gives you access to a great deal of information. That access, however, comes with a price: vulnerability to crackers, viruses, spyware, and so on.

One of the best ways to protect yourself is to modify your own behavior. Just as you would not give personal information to a stranger on the street, you must learn to protect your identity and information online.

In addition, tools are available to help you make your laptop secure. For example, you can set a password, install firewall software or an antivirus program, and so on.

Crackers

Crackers are constantly developing new ways to exploit the Internet for ill gain. Some crackers create viruses, which are programs designed with some malicious intent; others use keystroke-tracking software to follow you around online; still others gather information that you contribute to blogs or social sites to steal your identity. Note that crackers should not be confused with hackers. Where crackers exploit technology for ill gain, hackers simply enjoy the challenge involved in breaking into computer systems. Unlike crackers, hackers do no harm. In fact, true hackers subscribe to a strict code of ethics and frown upon crackers.

Viruses

A virus is a program created with malicious intent to copy itself and infect computers. Many viruses are distributed via e-mail, although some are downloaded alongside other files. Viruses can have a range of effects, from destroying data on your hard drive, to making changes in your operating system to open up a security gap, to making copies of a file until your laptop's memory is overwhelmed. Although the term *virus* is sometimes used to refer to other types of hostile, intrusive, or annoying software or code such as worms, Trojan horses, spyware, and so on, only self-replicating programs can truly be called viruses.

Spyware

Spyware is a type of malicious software, or *malware*, that attaches to other software that you download and installs itself on your computer. Spyware can take control of your laptop without your knowledge, collecting little bits of information about you as you work. For example, spyware might collect personal information that you would prefer to keep private, such as your Internet surfing habits. More than that, though, spyware can perform such nefarious tasks as redirecting your browser to a bogus Internet site, where you might be prompted to enter personal information, or installing unwanted software on your laptop. Spyware may also result in unwanted pop-up ads appearing on your laptop.

Behavior

When using your laptop to surf the Internet, be careful where you go. Just as you do not walk in the worst part of town at midnight, so, too, should you avoid the unsavory parts of the Web. If you choose to register with a site and provide personal information, make sure that the site is secure and that they do not make your information public. Submit information or purchase items online only at sites that you trust. Do not post personal information on a public blog or other site. Information about your location, your family, your income, or your activities can provide what a predator needs to locate, stalk, or rob you.

Password

You can set up your laptop to require a password to log in. By setting a password, you prevent others who do not know your password from logging in to your Windows 7 laptop and accessing your files. Be sure to set a strong password to prevent others from cracking it. Your password should be at least eight characters long, should be a mixture of uppercase and lowercase letters, and should not contain your username, your real name, your company's name, or any complete words. Also, it is a good idea to periodically change your password. If you are worried you will forget your password, you can write it down, but be sure to store the written password somewhere safe and private.

Firewall

A firewall is a software program that stops certain types of data from passing from the Internet to your laptop (and vice versa) while still allowing other types of data to pass through. All data traveling between your laptop and the Internet passes through the firewall; the firewall examines each piece of data to determine whether it should be allowed to pass, blocking any data that does not meet the specified security criteria. A firewall is meant to help prevent intruders from accessing the data on your laptop via the Internet. Windows 7 includes its own firewall, called Windows Firewall, for use on your laptop.

Antivirus Software

Antivirus software, such as Norton AntiVirus, McAfee, and the free Microsoft Security Essentials, can be installed and set up to run regular scans for malware, including viruses, worms, and Trojan horses. Some antivirus software is also designed to scan for spyware and adware. (Adware is software installed on a computer, usually without the user's knowledge, that automatically displays advertisements.) Be sure to regularly run the Update Virus Definitions feature, because new viruses appear all the time. Keep in mind that antivirus and antispyware programs use system resources, which may be a reason to buy a laptop with extra RAM and CPU processing speed.

Password-Protect Your Laptop

If you care about keeping your files private, creating a password is crucial. Doing so prevents anyone who does not know the password from logging on to your account and accessing your files.

Setting a strong password is important — that is, one that is at least eight characters long; does not contain your username, your real name, your company's name, or any complete words; and contains a mixture of uppercase and lowercase letters, numbers, symbols, and spaces. For an added layer of protection, consider changing your password periodically. If you write down your password, be sure to store it somewhere safe and private.

① In the main Control Panel window, click **User Accounts and Family Safety**.

Note: To open the Control Panel window, click the **Start** button (⊞) and click **Control Panel**.

The User Accounts and Family Safety window opens.

② Under User Accounts, click **Change your Windows password**.

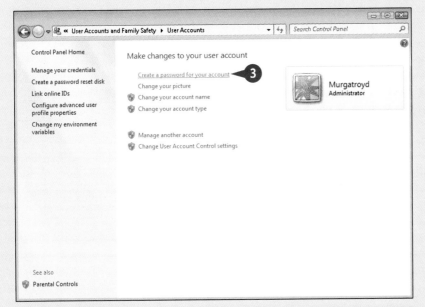

The User Accounts screen opens.

3 Click **Create a password for your account**.

4 Type the password you want to use in the topmost field.

5 Type the password a second time in the next field to confirm it.

6 Type a password hint in the next field.

Note: *If you forget your password, press* Enter *when Windows 7 displays the Welcome screen to view your password hint.*

7 Click **Create password**.

Windows 7 password-protects the user account.

Simplify It

How do you set up Windows to require a password when it wakes from Sleep mode?
To set up Windows to require a password when your laptop wakes from Sleep mode, click **Hardware and Sound** in the Control Panel window; then, under Power Options, click **Require a password on wakeup**. The System Settings screen appears. Select the **Require a Password** option button and click **Save changes**.

What if you forget your password?
If you forget your password, you must reset it using an Administrator account. If you forget the password for an Administrator account and no other Administrator accounts are on the laptop, you must reinstall Windows, which means you will lose all your files.

Encrypt Your Data

If someone gains access to your files via a network, you can prevent that person from viewing the files' contents by encrypting them.

You can use the Windows 7 Encrypting File System, or EFS, to encrypt any files or folders that you store on your drive. With EFS, you choose what files and folders you want to encrypt. When you encrypt an entire folder, you automatically encrypt all of the files and subfolders within it. EFS works by issuing a file encryption key, which EFS then uses to encrypt and decrypt your data.

Note that to run EFS, your laptop must be running Windows 7 Professional, Enterprise, or Ultimate Edition.

Encrypt Your Data

① In Windows Explorer, right-click the file or folder you want to encrypt.

② Click **Properties**.

Note: Not all files and folders can be encrypted. For example, compressed files or folders and system files that support your operating system cannot be encrypted.

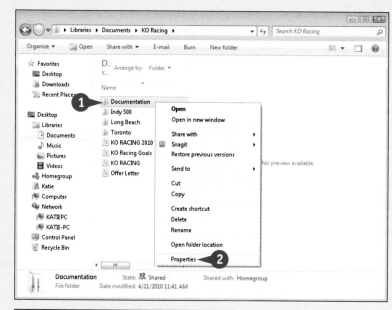

The file or folder's Properties dialog box opens.

③ If necessary, click the **General** tab.

④ Click **Advanced**.

● The Advanced Attributes dialog box opens.

⑤ Click the **Encrypt contents to secure data** check box (☑) to select it.

⑥ Click **OK**.

⑦ Click **OK**.

If you are encrypting a folder, the Confirm Attribute Changes dialog box opens, asking whether the encryption should be applied to the folder only or to subfolders and files in the folder.

If you are encrypting a file, the Encryption Warning dialog box opens, asking if you want to encrypt the file and its parent folder or just the file.

⑧ Select the desired option (◉).

⑨ Click **OK**.

What if your encryption key is deleted or corrupted?
If your encryption key is deleted or corrupted, your data will be impossible to recover. For this reason, after you encrypt a file or folder, it is critical that you back up your encryption key; store the backup on removable media such as a USB flash drive, a CD or DVD, or an external hard drive; and keep this media in a safe place. You can also create a recovery certificate to recover files. For help backing up your encryption key and creating a recovery certificate, see the Help information in Windows 7.

Thwart Intruders with Windows Firewall

If your laptop is connected to the Internet, it is vulnerable to such dangers as crackers, Internet worms, and more. To protect your system, you can enable Windows Firewall, which creates a barrier between your private computer files and outside connections.

When you enable Windows Firewall, it monitors all programs that access the Internet from your

computer or try to communicate with you from an external source and moves to block programs that may compromise the security of your system. When this happens, Windows Firewall displays a message asking what you want to do; you can choose to either continue blocking the software or stop blocking it.

Thwart Intruders with Windows Firewall

Enable Windows Firewall

① In the main Control Panel window, click **System and Security**.

*Note: To open the Control Panel window, click the **Start** button (⊞) and click **Control Panel**.*

The System and Security window opens.

② Click **Windows Firewall**.

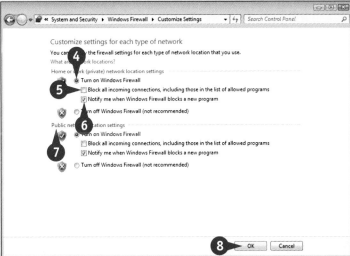

The Windows Firewall window opens.

③ Click **Turn Windows Firewall on or off**.

The Customize Settings screen appears.

④ Under Home or work (private) network location settings, select the **Turn on Windows Firewall** option button (◉).

⑤ Deselect the **Block all incoming connections** check box (☐).

⑥ Select the **Notify me when Windows Firewall blocks a new program** check box (☑).

⑦ Repeat Steps **4** to **6** under Public network location settings.

⑧ Click **OK**.

Windows 7 enables Windows Firewall.

What about physical threats?
Because of their small size and the fact that they are portable, laptops are especially vulnerable to physical threats such as theft as well as prying eyes. Various tools can protect your laptop from these threats. For example, you can install a fingerprint reader; that way, you can use your finger, rather than a password, to gain access to your system. To prevent theft, you can buy a cable lock. You can then use it to lock your laptop to a stationary object such as a chair. Another option is to install tracking software to help you track your lost or stolen laptop.

continued

Thwart Intruders with Windows Firewall *(continued)*

Sometimes, Windows Firewall works a little *too* well. That is, it blocks a safe program or connection. For example, the firewall may block the short-term connection made when you attempt to instant-message with someone.

One way to deal with this is to temporarily disable the firewall. Doing so increases your system's exposure to various security threats, however. A better approach is to allow the problematic network connection or program as an exception. An *exception* is a program or connection that you want to allow so that it does not limit your ability to work or communicate.

Thwart Intruders with Windows Firewall *(continued)*

Manage Exceptions

1 In the main Control Panel window, click **System and Security**.

> **Note:** To open the Control Panel window, click the **Start** button (🔲) and click **Control Panel**.

2 In the System and Security window, under Windows Firewall, click **Allow a program through Windows Firewall**.

The Allow programs to communicate through Windows Firewall screen appears.

3 Click **Change settings**.

4 In the Allowed programs and features section, select a program or feature option (☐ changes to ☑).

Note: *To block rather than allow a program or feature, uncheck the check box next to the program or feature you want to block.*

5 In the program's or feature's Home/Work (Private) and Public section, select (☑) or deselect (☐) options to indicate whether the program or feature should be enabled on both types of networks.

6 Click **OK**.

Simplify It

What other forms of protection does your system need?
In addition to Windows Firewall, you should run antivirus software and be careful when opening e-mail attachments or other files from any source, even a trusted one, to avoid inadvertently infecting your system with a virus. Norton and McAfee are two companies that sell reliable antivirus software.

What is Windows Defender?
Windows Defender is a program that runs automatically to scan for and uninstall spyware. *Spyware* is software installed on your computer, usually without your knowledge or consent, that can deluge your system with unwanted pop-up ads, and also monitor and record your Web-surfing activities and transmit this data to interested parties — including crackers.

Enable Windows 7 Parental Controls

If you share your laptop with children, you can set up the Windows 7 parental controls.

One way to use parental control is to limit children's use of the laptop to certain hours of the day on certain days of the week. If the child tries to log in at a restricted time,

Windows 7 blocks access; if the child is logged on at the commencement of the blocked time, Windows 7 automatically logs him or her off.

To implement the Windows 7 parental controls, each child who uses your computer must have his or her own Standard user account.

Enable Windows 7 Parental Controls

1 In the main Control Panel window, under User Accounts and Family Safety, click **Set up parental controls for any user**.

*Note: To open the Control Panel window, click the **Start** button (🔳) and click **Control Panel**.*

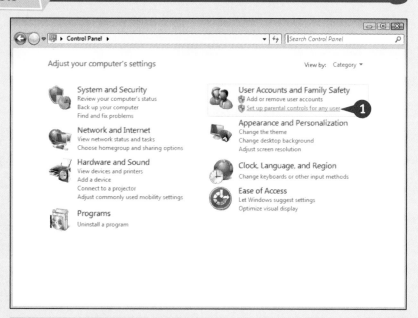

The Parental Controls window opens.

2 Click the user account to which you want to apply parental controls.

The User Controls window opens.

③ Under Parental Controls, click the **On, enforce current settings** option (◉) to select it.

④ Click **Time limits**.

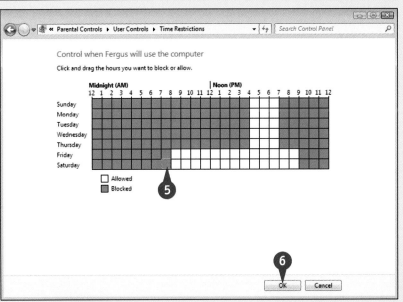

The Time Restrictions window opens.

⑤ Click and drag to indicate the hours during which you want to block or allow computer use for this account.

⑥ Click **OK**.

Simplify It

How do you create a Standard user account?
To implement the Windows 7 parental controls, children using your laptop must have their own Standard user accounts. To create a Standard user account, click the **Start** button and click **Control Panel**. Then, under **User Accounts and Family Safety**, click **Add or remove user accounts**. The Manage Accounts window opens; click **Create a new account**. In the Create New Account window, type a name for the new account, select the Standard account type, and click **Create Account**. Windows creates a Standard account. To log on to the account, click it in the Windows 7 Welcome screen.

continued

Enable Windows 7 Parental Controls *(continued)*

You can also use Windows 7 parental controls to restrict access to games on the computer. Games can be restricted by game rating, or on a game-by-game basis.

In addition, Windows 7 parental controls can be used to restrict access to programs you might prefer to keep private. For example, you might

choose to restrict access to a money-management program.

In addition to using Windows 7 parental controls to keep kids safe, you can use the Internet Explorer 8 Content Advisor feature to prevent exposure to inappropriate subject matter, such as violent or sexually explicit Internet content.

Enable Windows 7 Parental Controls *(continued)*

⑦ In the User Controls window, click **Games**.

The Game Controls window opens.

⑧ Under Can *X* Play Games?, click the **No** option (◎ changes to ◉) to prevent the user from playing any games.

*Note: To allow the user to play certain games, click **Yes** in step 8. Then click the **Set Game Ratings** link to block or allow games based on rating. If you want to block certain games, click the **Block or Allow Specific Games** link; The Game Overrides window appears, enabling you to specify which games should be blocked or allowed.*

⑨ Click **OK**.

10 In the User Controls window, click **Allow and block specific programs**.

The Application Restrictions window opens.

11 To limit the programs available to this user, click the **X can only use the programs I allow** option (⊙) to select it.

● Windows displays a list of programs installed on the laptop.

12 Click the check box (☑) for each program you want to allow.

● You can click **Check All** and then uncheck (☐) those programs you want to block.

13 Click **OK** to close the Application Restrictions window.

14 Click **OK** to return to the Parental Controls window.

Are there other ways to protect kids?
In addition to using the Windows 7 parental controls to limit access to games and programs, you can also use the parental controls included with Internet Explorer 8, called Content Advisor, to prevent exposure to inappropriate subject matter, such as violent or sexually explicit Internet content. To enable Content Advisor, click the **Tools** button in Internet Explorer 8 and click **Internet Options**. The Internet Options dialog box opens; click the **Content** tab and, under Content Advisor, click **Enable**. The Content Advisor dialog box opens; adjust the settings in the various tabs as desired and click **OK**.

Filter Spam and Scams

In addition to being a real time-waster, spam e-mails often involve scams, making spam potentially dangerous. You can use Windows Live Mail's junk e-mail filter to divert spam from your inbox into a special Junk e-mail folder. The Windows Live Mail junk e-mail filter is enabled by default, but moves only the most obvious junk e-mail messages into your Junk

e-mail folder. If you want, you can change the level of filtering.

You should occasionally check your Junk e-mail folder to make sure no legitimate messages were diverted there by accident. E-mails that are not junk can be moved to your inbox.

Filter Spam and Scams

Change the Filter Level

1 In Windows Live Mail, click the **Menus** button (🖳).

2 Click **Safety options**.

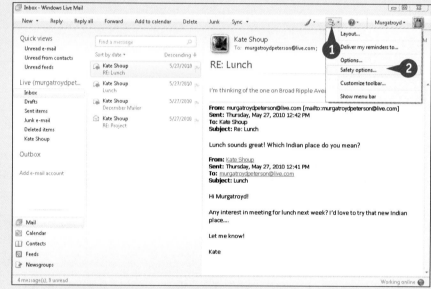

The Safety Options dialog box opens with the Options tab displayed.

3 Select the desired level of protection.

🔵 Click **No Automatic Filtering** if you do not want to block any junk e-mail messages.

🔵 Click **Low** to block only the most obvious spam.

🔵 Click **High** to block yet more suspected spam.

⚪ Click **Safe List Only** to block all messages except those from people or domains on your Safe Senders list.

4 Click **OK**.

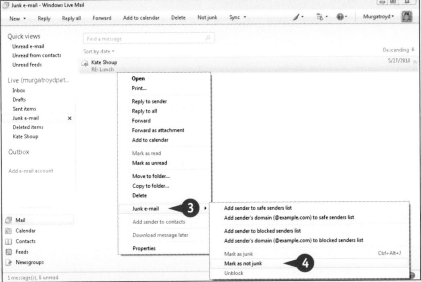

Mark Mail as Not Junk

1 Click the **Junk e-mail** folder in the Windows Live folder list.

● Messages diverted to the Junk e-mail folder appear in the File list.

2 Right-click a message that is not junk.

3 Click **Junk e-mail**.

4 Click **Mark as not junk**.

The message is moved to your inbox.

Note: *To stop blocking messages from a sender, right-click a message from that sender, click **Junk e-mail**, click **Add sender to safe senders list**, and click **OK**.*

Note: *To automatically divert all messages from a sender to your Junk e-mail folder, right-click a message from the sender, click **Junk e-mail**, click **Add sender to blocked senders list**, and click **OK**.*

What is phishing?
Phishing is an attempt by a malicious party to obtain private information from computer users. Often, phishing involves an e-mail message that appears to be from a legitimate source such as a bank that contains links that direct users to a bogus Web site designed to steal personal information. If you use a Windows Live or Hotmail account with Windows Live Mail, the program automatically checks the sender ID of all incoming messages in an attempt to detect phishing messages. In addition, the Internet Explorer 8 SmartScreen Filter, enabled by default, helps detect fraudulent Web sites.

Index

Index

Index

Index